Pioneers
and
Trailblazers
ADVENTURES OF THE OLD WEST

Pioneers and Trailblazers

ADVENTURES OF THE OLD WEST

6 VOLUMES IN 1

INDIANS, PIONEERS, COWBOYS, RAILROADERS, GUNFIGHTERS, SOLDIERS

Written by Leonard J. Matthews
Illustrated by Geoffrey Campion and others
Edited by Arlene Rourke

DERRYDALE BOOKS
New York

This 1990 edition is published by Derrydale Books,
distributed by Outlet Book Company, Inc,
a Random House Company,
225 Park Avenue South, New York, New York 10003,
by arrangement with Rourke Publications, Inc.

Manufactured in the United States of America

Library of Congress Cataloging-in-Publication Data

Matthews, Leonard, 1920-
Pioneers and trailblazers : adventures of the Old West / by
Leonard J. Matthews.
    p.   cm.
"Originally published in six separate volumes: The Wild West in
American history: Soldiers; Indians; Pioneers; Cowboys; Railroaders;
Gunfighters"—T.p. verso.
Summary: Examines the exploration and settlement of the West
through the experiences of settlers, gunfighters, cowboys, Indians,
trailblazers, and soldiers.
1. Frontier and pioneer life—West (U.S.)—Juvenile literature.
2. West (U.S.)—History—Juvenile literature. [1. Frontier and
pioneer life—West (U.S.) 2. West (U.S.)—History.] I. Title.
            F596.M337   1990
        978—dc20   90-32399
                CIP
                AC

ISBN 0-517-02537-X
8 7 6 5 4 3 2 1

CONTENTS

INDIANS

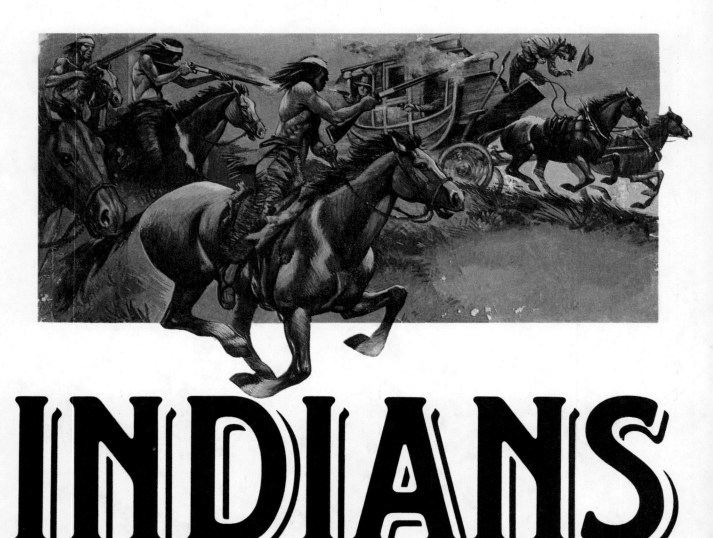

INDIANS

It is a well-known fact that when Christopher Columbus first set foot on a little island in the year 1492, he believed he had reached India.

Columbus, though, was mistaken. He had not landed in India. He had arrived at an island that he named San Salvador. There is still argument as to which island it really was, but it is generally thought to have been one of the Bahama Islands, north east of Cuba and south of Florida.

Columbus mistakenly called the natives of this newly discovered continent Indians. For some reason, the name stuck. To this day, descendants of the people who were living in the Americas are usually referred to as Indians.

For almost 300 years after Columbus landed, the Indians fought the white invaders for the land that they rightfully believed was theirs. Not until December 1890 did they finally submit when 144 Sioux, men, women and children, died under the guns of their old enemy, the U.S. 7th Cavalry.

The story that follows relates some of the adventures of the most famous leaders of the Western tribes. They were all gallant men who were always prepared to lay down their lives for their just cause.

WAR TO THE DEATH

To the first white men who came to America, the natives seemed to be living little better than stone age people. These European explorers saw only what the natives did not have; they did not notice or appreciate their rich culture.

At that time the Indians had no horses. There were no horses on the American continent. The Indians' utensils and weapons were made of grass, clay, wood, and stone. They fought and hunted with wooden bows and arrows and stone hatchets.

These natives were clever hunters, even though they had to hunt on foot. They knew the ways and habits of the animals they killed for food.

The arrival of the Europeans, particularly the conquistadores from Spain, must have shocked the simple Indians. These newcomers were greedy for gold and jewels, and the conquistadores were ruthless in their search for plunder. In no time they had turned the Indians into their enemies. Yet unknowingly the Spanish brought to the natives a great treasure: horses.

At first the natives thought that a mounted man and his horse were one animal. As soon as they understood that they were two separate beings and that horses could be mounted and used in the hunt, the Indians wanted them. They did their best to obtain as many as possible. They often bartered rich furs or gold nuggets for horses. Sometimes they just stole them instead.

Once they were mounted, the Plains Indians could hunt their favorite prey, the buffalo, more easily. The buffalo, also called the

Horses were the Indians' dearest possessions. If they could not buy them, they would steal them.

The bison (or buffalo as it is more generally known) provided the Indians with food, clothes, ornaments and weapons.

American bison, provided an Indian with all he needed: food, clothes, ornaments, and even some of his weapons. The Indians used every part of the buffalo in one way or another.

To the Plains Indians, buffalo was of vital importance. Should they be deprived of this animal, their way of life, and perhaps their very existence, was threatened. When white hunters started to kill off the great herds of buffalo, the Indians were outraged. Thousands of buffalo were killed to provide food for the Chinese and Irish workers who were laying railroad tracks across the country. The meat was eaten, but the remainder of the animal was wasted. The Indians saw this as a tragic loss.

In addition, thousands of settlers and ex-soldiers began pouring into the lands where they lived. To try to retain what was theirs, many Indian tribes took to the warpath. They were convinced that their only hope was to wipe out every white hunter, every white pioneer, and every paleface long-knife soldier who dared to enter their hunting grounds.

For the most part, it was war to the death between Indians and white invaders in the American West.

RED CLOUD AND CRAZY HORSE STRIKE

T he U.S. Government often tried to adopt the appearance of fair dealing with the Indians. They drew up treaties in which they promised small sums of money to the Indians for Indian lands. If certain tribes were on the verge of attack, the government drew up treaties guaranteeing the Indians proper ownership of their territory. This was an admission on the part of the white government that the land did belong to the Indian people.

White people seldom kept their promises. Each time they broke treaties, they planted more bitterness in the hearts of the Indians who believed that the land belonged to God, to Manitou, the Great Spirit. No human had any more right to it than did the animals roaming the wide open spaces. The idea that land could be bought and sold was the white man's thinking. Indians entered into the treaties because they thought that this was the only way they could have peace.

Perhaps that was why Red Cloud, head war chief of the Sioux, agreed to a new treaty drawn up by the American Government. This treaty stated that the hunting grounds of the Sioux, Cheyennes, and Arapahos should remain their land forever and that no white settler should ever set foot on their territory.

This stretch of beautiful country lay between the Black Hills, the Rocky Mountains, and Yellowstone River. The Powder River ran through it, and the land was full of game.

The day came in 1866, however, when Red Cloud reined his sleek pony on the crest of a hill. He looked grimly down on the newly built army post of Fort Phil Kearny on the Bozeman Trail in what is today northern Wyoming. Red

This photo was taken during an Indian delegation to Washington, D.C. The Indians (l. to r.) are Red Dog, Little Wound, Red Cloud, American Horse and Red Shirt. (Photo: National Archives, Washington, D.C.)

Red Cloud, who was the head war chief of the Sioux Indians. *(Photo: National Archives, Washington, D.C.)*

Cloud's heart was full of hatred and bitterness, for once again the United States Government had broken its treaty. It had built a string of forts across the Indians' hunting grounds.

This time the Government's excuse was gold. Gold had been discovered in Idaho and Montana, and miners had at once headed for the gold fields.

By far the easiest and quickest route lay through the Indians' territory. The Government tried to make a new agreement with the Sioux and Cheyenne to build a road across their hunting grounds. The Indians refused. They knew that their lands would be overrun with land-grabbing white people. Within a short time, they would be driven out of their own territory.

With no regard for the Indians, the Government broke the treaty and ordered several forts to be built along the Bozeman Trail. These would protect the whites flocking to the gold fields.

In spite of many protests and warnings by the Indians, the forts were erected. Fort Phil Kearny was completed in the autumn of 1866.

While it was being built, Red Cloud and his warriors continually harassed the men, stealing horses, sniping and raiding supply wagons. They had done all they could to drive the soldiers away. When every effort failed, Red Cloud vowed to wage a full-scale war. He would attack the fort and destroy it.

As he gazed down on the army post, a majestic young warrior drew rein beside him. This was Crazy Horse, Red Cloud's fighting chief. He too, like Red Cloud, was an Oglala Sioux.

Indian chiefs were not as important as some novels and Hollywood films suggest. A brave was never obliged to fight. His "medicine" might be bad on a certain day. If he did not feel lucky, he would remain in his tepee. Thus a chief might set out on the warpath without a full muster of warriors. Nevertheless, Crazy Horse vowed to set a trap for the white pony soldiers the very next day.

The following morning was bitterly cold. The land was covered with a blanket of frost encrusted snow. It was December 21, 1866. A group of loggers left the fort and headed for the hillside to fell trees and saw logs. There were families in the fort, as well as officers and men, and much fuel was needed to keep the place warm. Suddenly a band of warriors swooped down on the wagons of the loggers.

On hearing shots, a young captain named William Fetterman swiftly led 80 cavalrymen out of the fort and raced to the assistance of the loggers. At once the Indians turned and fled. Fetterman galloped after them with his cavalrymen close behind. In doing so he disobeyed the orders of his commanding officer at the fort, Colonel Henry Carrington.

Carrington was wise in the cunning of the Indians. Fetterman, fresh from a brilliant career during the Civil War, was not. He led his men over a ridge in hot pursuit of the small band of Indians, straight into an ambush skillfully planned by Crazy Horse. Hundreds of Sioux, Cheyenne, and Arapaho warriors leaped from hiding places and let loose volleys of arrows with deadly accuracy.

Fetterman and his gallantly fighting soldiers were all dead after thirty minutes of hand-to-hand fighting. From that day forward the ridge on which they fought was known as Massacre Hill.

That night, a civilian scout, John "Portugee" Phillips, set out to ride 236 miles through blinding snow blizzards to Fort Laramie. He arrived there, completely exhausted, on Christmas night. He gasped out the news that Fort Kearny was being attacked by Indians. Two days later the relief force left Fort Laramie and headed for Fort Kearny.

In temperatures ranging between 25 and 45 degrees below zero, the relief force journeyed through raging snowstorms and drifts three feet deep. They finally reached Fort Kearny three weeks later.

After that the fort was under constant seige. Eight months later, Crazy Horse launched a fullscale attack on Fort Kearny. Nearly 2,000 painted warriors charged the fort. The soldiers, now armed with the latest breech-loading Springfield .55 caliber rifles, managed eventually to beat off the Indian assault.

Due to the bitter weather, Red Cloud and his warriors had not attempted another attack on the fort. They remained nearby, though, and were still determined to destroy it.

The fort remained under siege and continual harassment by Crazy Horse and his warriors for nearly a year. At last the garrison of Fort Kearny could stand the pressure no longer. The post was abandoned in August 1868.

Red Cloud and Crazy Horse watched the soldiers and their families leave. They were still in sight of the fort when Red Cloud gave the order to set the building on fire. Not until the fort was a smoldering mass of ashes and the last white soldier had disappeared from view, did Red Cloud and Crazy Horse wheel their ponies and ride away.

Red Cloud continued to be the leader and spokesman for the Oglala Teton Sioux and forsook the warpath. In November 1868 he signed a peace treaty with the U.S. Government. Two years later he was invited to Washington, where he had two meetings with President Ulysses S. Grant.

For the rest of his life, though, he hated the

Crazy Horse vowed to Red Cloud that he would set a trap next day for the soldiers of Fort Kearny.

7

white men. "They made us many promises," he said, "more than I can remember. They kept only one. They promised to take our land and they took it."

Red Cloud died in 1909 at the age of 87. As for Crazy Horse, he went on to lead the Oglala Sioux. They overwhelmed General George Armstrong Custer and his 264 troopers on the banks of the Little Big Horn River on June 25, 1876.

It was Crazy Horse of the Oglala Sioux who led the tribesmen who overwhelmed Custer and his troopers at the Battle of the Little Big Horn.

The following year, Crazy Horse with 2,000 warriors surrendered to the U.S. Cavalry. A few months later he was charged with causing more trouble. He attempted to escape and was killed by Private William Gentles, who stabbed the war chief with his bayonet. That night, September 5, 1877, Crazy Horse died. He was only 35 years old.

THE WARPATH OF THE NEZ PERCE

*N*ot until 1863 did the Nez Perce, a peace-loving tribe of Indians, fight the white invaders of their land. They lived between the Blue Mountains in Oregon and the Bitter Root Mountains in Idaho.

They called themselves "The People." The name Nez Perce (pronounced nay per-say by the French but now commonly pronounced nezz purse) is French for "pierced noses." Only one small branch of the tribe actually pierced their noses. In 1835 this tribe came in contact with some French Canadian trappers who gave the name to the entire tribe.

When the white men came to their land, the Nez Perce welcomed them. They were open to new ideas, and greeted the missionaries and traders with open arms. The Nez Perce helped the white settlers to build a blacksmith shop and a saw mill. Many of them embraced the Christian religion. Three chiefs who had been converted signed a treaty with the United States at the great Walla-Walla Council of 1855. The Government treaty spelled out the boundaries of their territories. But it did not guarantee the Indians protection from land speculators and prospectors.

Trouble broke out when a prospector from California discovered gold in the Clearwater region of the Nez Perce hunting grounds. Miners began to pour into the territory.

Chief Joseph of the Nez Perce Indians. *(Photo: Bureau of American Ethnology).*

The Nez Perce were divided on the mining issue. Some chiefs wished to protect their lands and keep the miners out at all costs. Other chiefs were persuaded or bribed into allowing a certain amount of prospecting. It was a fatal move.

Gold fever brought thousands of speculators to the region. Tent towns sprang up overnight and soon steamboats were churning up the Columbia and Snake Rivers, laden with supplies for the miners. They swarmed all over the Nez Perce hunting grounds disregarding treaties and agreements.

CHIEF JOSEPH'S FIGHTING RETREAT

*I*n 1863 the Commissioners of Indian Affairs, acting under pressure from the various business companies that were now holding sway in the territory, called the Nez Perce chiefs to a council. They had drawn up a treaty that called for the removal of the Nez Perce to a reservation. Chief Joseph of the Wallowa Band of Lower Nez Perce refused to sign the treaty and warned all white men to stay away from his hunting grounds. The council broke up with no agreement.

Five years later a delegation of Nez Perce chiefs went to Washington to sign a treaty, on behalf of their people, agreeing to removal. All they wanted was a strip of land where they could live in peace.

Chief Joseph was not among them. He still stubbornly refused to give up the lands of his forefathers.

Other Nez Perce chiefs, among them Looking Glass and White Bird, also opposed the treaty and began to talk of war. Chief Joseph tried to restrain them, urging them to keep the peace no matter what the cost. "Better to live in peace than to begin a war and lie dead," he said. The pressures, however, were too great.

In June 1877, young Nez Perce warriors unable to contain their anger at their persecution any longer, painted themselves for war and raided along the Salmon River settlements, killing several pioneers. The countryside buzzed with news of the attack. Two companies of the First Cavalry, under Captain David Perry, were sent to protect the settlers. For the first time in their history, the Nez Perce were at war with the white men.

Chief Joseph had been so named by his white teacher, a missionary. His Indian name was Himmaton-Yalatkit, which means "Thunder Coming from the Water over the Land."

Joseph, now resigned to warfare, together with Chiefs Looking Glass, White Bird, and several warriors, waited for the cavalry in a canyon. The troopers rode straight into the ambush and were completely routed. Within minutes, the soldiers were riding for their lives

The Nez Perce Indians had always lived at peace with the white people until gold was discovered in the Indians' hunting grounds.

with a horde of screaming Indians hot on their heels.

Ten days later, the Indians learned that an army under the command of a one-armed U.S. General named Oliver Otis Howard was on the move. Joseph, Looking Glass, and White Bird soon discovered that their band of 300 warriors and their families were outnumbered ten to one. There was no hope now of saving their lands. The only course open to them was to cross the Bitter Root Mountains and escape to Canada.

Joseph did not like the idea of retreating. "What are we fighting for?" he asked. "Is it for our lives? No. It is for the land where the bones of fathers are buried. I do not want to die in a strange land. Remain with me here and we shall have plenty of fighting. Let us die on our own land."

He was outvoted. The Indians prepared to travel the long trail of 250 miles over the Bitter Root Mountains. The women and children gathered roots and berries for food. Rear and advance guards of warriors were on watch, and every man had a string of spare horses.

Then the fugitives set out, over winding ridges and along sudden precipices, through tangled undergrowth and pine forests. Some Indians were lost as they ventured across rock slides. Horses stumbled and fell as they tried to follow the tortuous paths.

The army anticipated the move Joseph made. General Howard followed the Nez Perce while another force moved in to block the Indians' path at the north end of the trail.

Joseph quietly eluded both forces and crossed the mountains safely into Montana. The weary travelers made camp on August 8 at the

Big Hole Basin. The next day they rested, but later that night they were attacked by a strong force of U.S. troopers under the command of Colonel John Gibbon. The Indians were taken completely by surprise but fought back valiantly. All night they battled hand-to-hand. The next morning the soldiers began to retreat, only to regroup and dig in. A great wail went up from the Indians' encampment. The ground was littered with the bodies of women and children who had died in the night attack. Among them was Chief Joseph's wife.

Army reinforcements were soon moving in the direction of the Big Hole Basin and once again the Nez Perce band turned north. Every turn they made was blocked by soldiers as the army bore down on the Indians. The ranks of the Nez Perce warriors were now thinning rapidly as they fought skirmish after skirmish with the soldiers.

Winter was closing in fast, and the Indians were exhausted by the months of pursuit and battle. The women and children suffered badly in the terrible cold. Fatigue and hunger weakened them still further. On and on through the snowswept Bear Paw Mountains they struggled. The old ones died by the wayside.

Only 30 miles from the Canadian border, a cavalry column under General Nelson Miles encircled the Nez Perce and attacked immediately. The Indians fought back, but during the fighting their horses were run off. Escape to Canada was made impossible.

General Miles had brought artillery with him, and now the big guns opened fire. The Indians fought on for another five days, firing from crude trenches, their wounded lying unattended. A raging blizzard enveloped them and added to their miseries.

On October 4, General Howard arrived with reinforcements, and for the Indians, all hope was gone. The next day, Chief Joseph surrendered. Only 87 warriors were still alive and half of these were wounded. He could not bear to see his people suffer any more. Handing his robe to General Miles he said: "I am tired of fighting. Our chiefs are killed. Looking Glass is dead. The old men are all dead. It is cold and we have no blankets. The little children are freezing to death. Hear me, I am tired. My heart is sick and sad. From where the sun now stands, I will fight no more forever."

Two years later the Nez Perce were herded onto a reservation in Oklahoma. Conditions were bad. There was no game to hunt, nor were there beautiful valleys and rich pastures for their horses. They were like babies, totally dependent on the Indian agent for their food. Exhaustion and sickness overtook them, and many died.

Joseph sent a petition to Washington, pleading for his people to be allowed to return to their lands. Then he added: "If I cannot go to my own home, let me have a home in some country where my people will not die so fast."

In May 1885 he and the Nez Perce survivors were allowed to return to the Northwest but not to Chief Joseph's beloved Wallowa Valley.

Joseph was a hero of the Indians and the white men alike. Yet still an exile from his lovely homeland, he died in 1904 on the Colville Reservation in Washington State.

A COMANCHE NAMED PARKER

*I*n 1836, a thirteen-year-old white girl named Cynthia Ann Parker was kidnapped. A band of Comanche Indians took her during a raid on Parker's Fort on the banks of the Navasota River in Texas.

One of the most ruthless of the Comanche chiefs, Peta Nocona, later took Cynthia as his wife. They had two sons, Quanah and Pecos, and a daughter, Topasannah.

Fifteen years after her capture by the Comanches, Cynthia Ann was taken prisoner by a company of U.S. troopers and Texan settlers when they raided Peta Nocona's camp. At the time Peta Nocona and his warriors had gone

The Comanches raided forts and ranches throughout Kansas, Texas, Colorado, and New Mexico.

hunting. The raiders slew many Comanche women. They were about to kill Cynthia Ann when a Texas Ranger noticed her fair hair.

With her little daughter, Cynthia Ann was returned to her uncle, Isaac Parker, a rancher who had served with the U.S. Army. Her husband and two sons were not captured. They managed to escape into the boundless prairie.

Four years later, Cynthia's daughter died of a fever and the mother, stricken with grief, starved herself to death. Meanwhile Quanah Parker became a brilliant warrior under his chieftain father's guidance. When Peta Nocona died, Quanah became chief in his stead.

Quanah is a strange name for a fighting Comanche chief because it means "fragrant." The name was given to him by his mother, and Quanah refused steadfastly to change it. As Quanah Parker, he is renowned in the history of the Plains Indians of the old West. In 1871, when Quanah was 26 years old, Captain Ronald Mackenzie led a troop of U.S. cavalry on a special mission. He had been ordered to put an end to Comanche raids led by Quanah Parker.

If he hoped to surprise Quanah, he was mistaken. He and his men were bedded down for the night when, without warning, Quanah led his warriors in a headlong charge through Mackenzie's camp. The warriors fired into the air, stampeding the troopers' horses. Yelling with triumph, the Comanches rode off with as many horses as they could round up.

Ronald Mackenzie swore that one day he would have his revenge. His chance came three years later, in 1874. Several Comanches, Kiowas, and Cheyennes were camped in Palo Duro Canyon. Quite unexpectedly Mackenzie, now a colonel, happened to come upon them.

Quanah Parker had been leading his warriors through one territory after another — Kansas, Texas, Colorado, New Mexico. The Comanches enriched themselves at the expense of unsuspecting ranchers and settlers. They lost few men during their exploits and could congratulate themselves on the many horses and the amount of plunder that fell into their hands.

At last, the Government issued instructions to the Army that the Comanches were to be rounded up and forced to live on reservations. Troops poured into Comanche territory from all directions. Out of Fort Concho in Texas came Colonel Mackenzie, burning to avenge his defeat at the hands of Quanah Parker. Without delay he ordered his men to attack. His main aim was to drive off all the horses. Without them, the Comanches could be tracked down and captured without much difficulty. The attack was successful and the troopers drove off fourteen horses. Then while the infuriated Comanches watched helplessly, the soldiers drove the horses to a ridge above the Indian encampment and killed them all.

The soldiers had slain only a few Indians, but Quanah Parker knew that the days of the Comanche warpath were over. Elsewhere white soldiers captured one band of Comanches after another.

In 1875 Quanah led the survivors of his tribe to a reservation and surrendered. From then on he encouraged his people to follow the "white man's way." He did all he could to explain to them the importance of education and how much more comfortable it was to live in houses rather than in tepees. Perhaps his most difficult task was trying to persuade them to take up agriculture and forsake the warpath forever.

He was 66 years old when he died in 1911 near Fort Sill, Oklahoma. He and his mother today lie buried in the old military cemetery at Fort Sill.

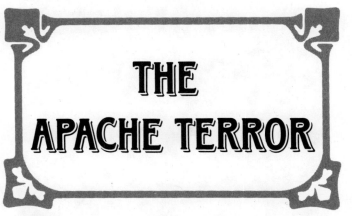

THE APACHE TERROR

Four hundred years ago, the Spanish conquistadores were riding northwards exploring California in search of gold and any other plunder. They also intended to establish missions and enslave the Indians. They came face to face with warriors who taught the cold-blooded Spaniards a lot about savagery, torture, and, above all, bravery against all odds.

The Spaniards called these ruthless tribesmen Coyoteros because they were as cunning as coyotes. The Zuni Indians though, called them Apache, meaning enemy. Enemies they were, as the other tribes already knew. The Spaniards and later white settlers paid a heavy price to discover this fact.

The United States began to take an interest in Arizona when huge balls of silver were found there in 1836. Prospectors flocked to the southwest. These miners soon found themselves enmeshed in a series of bitter wars with the Apaches.

In the 200 years since their first contact with the Europeans, the Apaches had adapted themselves well to the barren lands. Water and vegetation were scarce and few white men could survive in the landscape of volcanic rocks and blistering deserts.

Eight or more tribes were called by the general name of Apache. The most important were the Mescalero, Jicarilla, Mimbreños, Chiricahua, and Kiowa. The Chiricahua and several other tribes were grouped together and known as White Mountain Apaches.

No matter what their names, though, they were all pitiless, crafty, and distrustful. War was their business. They raided to obtain loot and slaves.

The young men of the tribe underwent a rigid initiation into the ranks of the warriors. They learned to stand and face the older braves who shot arrows at them. They had to dodge the arrows — or die.

When the sun was at its height, their mouths were filled with water and they were forced to run a course of many miles through difficult country. When they had finished their run, they had to spit out the water to show that they had not weakened and swallowed any.

They learned how to vanish like will o' the wisps in country that seemed to offer no cover and to strike where the enemy least expected them.

In the 1840s American settlers were pushing their way deeper into Arizona and New Mexico. Gold and silver strikes brought eager prospectors. To begin with the Apaches were not openly hostile. They hated the Spaniards and despised the Mexicans, but they approached the newcomers with curiosity.

One day, a group of miners, annoyed and suspicious of the Indians who persistently hung around their camp, seized one of them and tied him on the back of a wagon. They flogged him and drove him from their camp.

It was a recklessly stupid act, and the repercussions were terrifying. The man they had flogged was Mangus Colorado, a chief of the Mimbreños and related by marriage to chiefs of the Chiricahua and White Mountain bands.

For the rest of his life, Mangus Colorado made war. Mexicans, Spaniards, Americans — it mattered little. All the white men were his enemies.

The United States moved soldiers into the southwest and relations with the Apaches grew worse. White men hanged Apaches in retaliation for their raids. Apaches tortured white men to avenge the hangings.

In 1861, the Civil War broke out and the army garrisons in the southwest were recalled. At once the Apaches rampaged through the settlements, driving out the settlers and then destroying the homesteads.

Mangus Colorado and Cochise, chief of the Chricahuas, swept the territory clean and drove settlers into Tucson. Not long after even that town was reduced to a mere 200 inhabitants.

In 1862, General James H. Carleton marched from California with 3,000 volunteers to restore order in the Southwest. He launched a campaign of Apache extermination.

Miners and settlers were encouraged to return to Arizona and were offered rewards for Apache-killing expeditions. Bounty money was offered for Apache scalps.

Invitations to "talk peace" were sent out to the Apaches. Some, less distrustful than others, were shot down on arrival. Even Mangus Colorado was half-convinced by the offer of peace treaties. He was now an old man, and perhaps he believed that the "white-eyes" would treat him with kindness, especially if he rode in completely alone. If this is so, he made a big mistake.

Old he might have been, but he was a big man, proud and unafraid. He made the "long-knife" soldiers look like pigmies as they surrounded him, with faces scowling and rifles cocked.

During the night, as the soldiers and the

Apache chief lay beside a campfire, the troopers heated their bayonets in the fire. They thrust the hot steel at Mangus Colorado's feet. When the chief at last protested, they shot him dead. The official report on the death of Mangus Colorado was that he had died while "trying to escape."

In spite of his ferocious campaign, General Carleton failed to conquer the Apaches. They were pushed further and further into their inaccessible mountain hideouts and driven to still greater acts of merciless savagery.

The war dragged on. By 1871, it had cost the United States Government $40 million and 1,000 lives. It had accomplished nothing.

In February 1871, 150 members of the tribe of Arivaipa Apaches, came into Fort Grant. Their leader, Eskiminzin, said that his people were tired. Weary of the continual warfare, they now wanted to live in peace. They were given a strip of land near Tucson.

Two months later, on April 18, a mob of settlers marched out of Tucson and sprang a surprise attack on the Apaches. One hundred and eight men and women were slain and 29 children taken and sold into slavery.

The massacre caused a national outcry. One hundred men who had taken part in the slaughter were arrested and tried. They were declared not guilty by the jury.

A worried government sent General George Crook to Arizona. He was an expert Indian fighter but also a humane man. He was sympathetic towards the Indians, and his policy was one of understanding and peace. By 1874, all the important tribes had been won over or rounded up. The Apaches forsook the warpath and settled on the reservations.

Various bands of Apaches ran wild along the border country.

GERONIMO REBELS

The Apaches tried to settle down to agency life. They planted crops, only to see them fail in the barren soil.

Many white agents swindled the Apaches out of supplies and made money illegally by selling reservation lands. The women and children grew hungry. The warriors drifted into apathy and drunkeness. Once proud warriors were made to wear metal tags like dogs. One by one the various bands left the reservations and ran wild along the border country.

It is now that the notorious chief Geronimo enters our story. He was a medicine man and chief of the Chiricahua Apaches. His Apache name was Goyathlay, which means "One Who Yawns." The Mexicans called him Geronimo.

In 1876 when he was 42, he led a runaway band into Mexico. The United States Government had ordered all Apaches onto the San Carlos Agency in Arizona. Some time later, Geronimo and his followers were rounded up and also taken to San Carlos. They settled for a time, but were always discontented.

Geronimo's answer was to take to the war-path again. Once more the army was sent out after him, and he was forced to surrender. Not

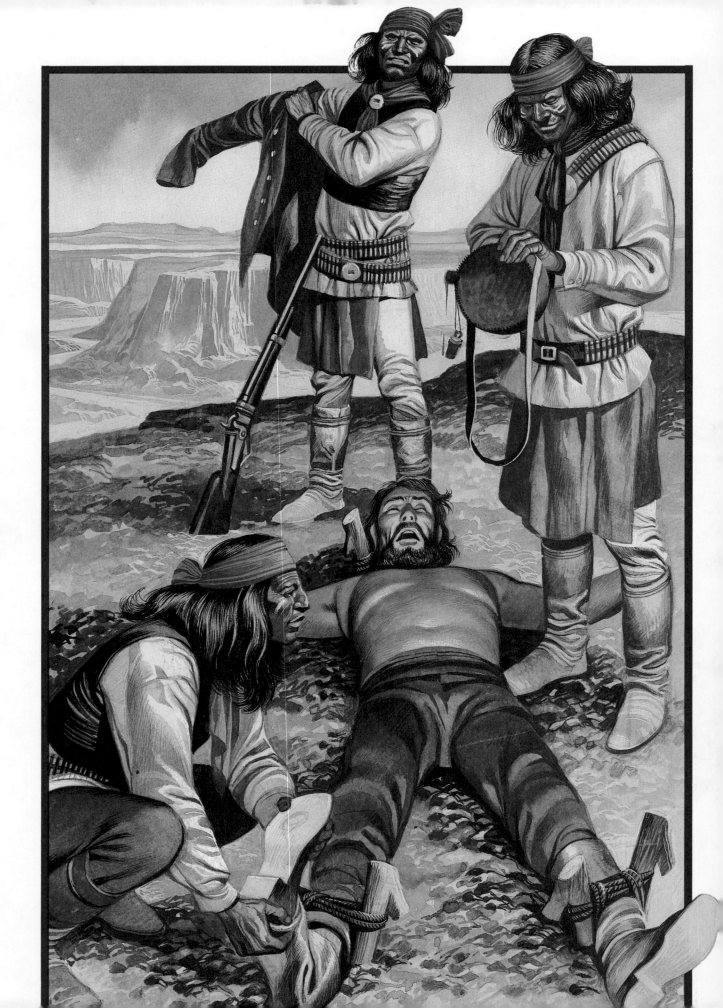

for long, though, did he live a peaceful life. The U.S. Government again forced him to forsake the ways of peace.

The Apaches liked drinking tiswin, a liquor which the Chiricahuas brewed from corn. The U.S. Government tried to ban the drink, because the Apaches became drunk and very troublesome when they drank tiswin.

Banning tiswin was enough reason for Geronimo to gather together a band of renegade Indians and once more ride the war trail. They raided white settlements in Arizona and Mexico and killed settlers. Any white men that fell into the hands of the Apaches were often tortured. Staking their victims out in the burning Arizona sun was a favorite Apache method of torture. General George A. Crook, a veteran Indian fighter, was ordered to capture or kill Geronimo and his warriors.

In March 1886, Geronimo and Crook met and arranged a treaty. Once more Geronimo broke away and headed for the border.

General Nelson A. Miles was dispatched to capture Geronimo. He formed the Apache Scouts and put Lt. Charles B. Gatewood in charge. Gatewood found out the location of Geronimo's camp and went in unarmed. He spent two days talking to Geronimo. In August 1886, Geronimo surrendered for the last time. He and 340 of his followers were taken to Florida. The old warrior was enslaved at hard labor for four years. He and his Chiricahuas were brought west again and settled in Fort Sill in Oklahoma.

He became a Christian and died a prisoner of war at Fort Sill in 1909. He was about 75. Geronimo was the last of the Apache war chiefs.

Above: **Geronimo, merciless enemy of the white men. (Photo: The Bettmann Archive).**

Left: **The Apaches would stake out their prisoners in the burning Arizona sun).**

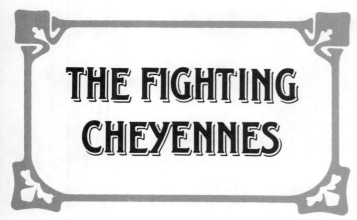

THE FIGHTING CHEYENNES

*L*ike the Nez Perce Indians, the Cheyennes were at first friendly toward the white people. In 1851, they attended the Great Council at Fort Laramie. There 10,000 Plains Indians signed an agreement with the U.S. Government and agreed to accept the territorial boundaries laid down in the treaties.

Once again the treaties were broken. As in the case of the Nez Perce, the discovery of gold and the resulting flood of miners caused the Cheyennes to take to the warpath.

Black Kettle, a chief of the Cheyennes, tried hard to preserve peace. He brought his people into Sand Creek, 40 miles northeast of Fort Lyon, Colorado. He even flew the Stars and Stripes over his tepee to show his loyalty.

At dawn on November 29, 1864, a band of Colorado Volunteers under the command of Colonel John M. Chivington, attacked the Cheyenne camp.

Many reasons have been given for this unprovoked attack. The Colorado miners hated the Cheyennes. But some people feel that it was a deliberate attempt to start an Indian war. The Colorado Volunteers would then have a reason to remain where they were and

would not be drawn into the Civil War that was then raging in the East.

Whatever the reason, the attack was a cold-blooded massacre. It was condemned by the entire nation. Cheyenne men, women, and children were ruthlessly shot down and killed. Black Kettle managed to escape, and the entire frontier erupted in warfare.

Custer led his 7th Cavalry into Black Kettle's village and slew more than 100 Cheyenne warriors.

Apaches, Kiowas, Comanches, Sioux, and Cheyennes took to the warpath. Colorado Territory was cut off from communication with the East. A campaign under General Winfield Scott Hancock failed to defeat the Indians. In 1868, General George Armstrong Custer took to the field with the 7th Cavalry.

In November 1868, Black Kettle and his followers were camped along the frozen Washita River. It was a hard winter and snow lay inches thick across the prairie. As the sky began to lighten, the still air was shattered by the sound of bugles, and Custer's 7th Cavalry came charging into the village. The Indians were taken completely by surprise. Black Kettle and more than a hundred of his warriors were slain.

For the next 10 years, the U.S. Army fought to subdue the Plains tribes. The Indian stood in the path of white man's progress. There was no longer room for him anywhere.

In 1865, the construction gangs of the Union Pacific and Kansas Pacific Rail roads began to inch their way across the Great Plains. Thousands of Irish immigrants set out to lay a mile of track each working day, and the steel rails began to eat into the prairies. The Iron Horse was sounding the death knell for the Cheyennes.

In 1870, leather factories in the East were offering high prices for buffalo hides. So buffalo hunters, including Buffalo Bill Cody, descended upon the herds and began to slaughter them in their thousands.

The buffalo was the mainstay of the Indians. Their lives depended on it. In one fateful decade millions of animals were cut down to a mere handful. Cheyenne warriors joined other Indians in derailing the trains and attacking the hunters. Now, they were fighting for survival against hopeless odds.

Then in 1876, the Cheyennes and the Sioux, whose chief medicine man was Sitting Bull, struck back with a vengeance. On June 25, hundreds of Indian warriors led by Crazy Horse drove Custer and his men up a slope of the Little Big Horn and slew them. Custer had paid in full for his pitiless attack on Black Kettle's camp eight years earlier.

A year later the Cheyennes agreed to surrender to the U.S. Army. General Crook held a council with the Cheyennes, and they agreed

George Armstrong Custer, doomed to die with his men at the Battle of the Little Big Horn. (Photo: National Archives, Washington, D.C.)

to give up their lands and move to a reservation in Oklahoma.

The new territory was far from their own hunting grounds. There were no buffalo, and game of any description was scarce. The Indians had to depend on the Indian agency to supply Texas cattle for food. Sickness overtook the Cheyennes, and they began to yearn for their own lands and their old way of life.

In July 1878, more than 300 Cheyennes left the reservation to "go home." The men,

23

women, and children were under the leadership of a chief named Dull Knife.

For six months the little band outwitted the thousands of soldiers sent to bring them in. Through blizzards and storms they struggled against overwhelming odds to reach their old hunting grounds.

On January 18, 1879, less than half of them reached the Platte River. There they surrendered to Lieutenant William P. Clark. General Crook petitioned the U.S. Government on their behalf, and they were given a reservation on the Tongue River and allowed to stay. There their descendants still live proudly as the Northern Cheyenne. They maintain close contact with others of their tribe in Oklahoma, the equally proud Southern Cheyenne.

In the days of their glory, no Indians were more respected by the white people than the "Fighting Cheyennes."

THE END OF THE WAR TRAIL

Sitting Bull, medicine man of the Hunkpapa Sioux. *(Photo: Smithsonian Institution, National Anthropological Archives, Washington, D.C.)*

Red Cloud and Crazy Horse were two very well-known Sioux chiefs. Equally well-known was a third chief. He was Sitting Bull, the medicine man and tribal chief of the Hunkpapa Sioux.

When he was 10 years old, he rode out on his first buffalo hunt. He was only 14 when he fought bravely in a skirmish with some Crow Indians. He was then known as Jumping Badger, but after his first fight he took the name of Four Horns.

For some reason he was not content with this name either. When he was 23 years of age, he became a medicine man and adopted the name of Sitting Buffalo Bull.

Sitting Bull was always involved with Sioux affairs. During the next 12 years, he became very important both as a warrior and adviser. At powwows his words were always listened to by the fighting chiefs.

His fame today, probably stems from his presence at the Battle of the Big Horn, Custer's Last Stand. On the day General Custer and his men were killed on the banks of the Little Big Horn River by a combined army of Sioux and Cheyennes, Sitting Bull was the Indian leader.

Although Sioux chiefs Crazy Horse and Gall were prominent during the battle, Sitting Bull was not. Later, it was said that he was off somewhere "making medicine." No one doubts, though, that Sitting Bull was a very brave Indian.

After the battle, Sitting Bull headed for the Canadian border with a large band of Sioux. There he believed he would be safe from the vengeance of pursuing U.S. cavalry.

He stayed in Canada for five years and then returned to the United States and surrendered. In 1885, he appeared in person with Buffalo Bill Cody in Cody's Wild West Show. People flocked to see the man who had defeated the great General Custer. When he rode into the arena during the performances, he was loudly hissed by audiences.

The medicine man, as it turned out, had not yet finished causing the white people trouble.

DEATH AT WOUNDED KNEE CREEK

The Indians were told that an Indian god would soon appear to help them defeat their enemies.

In 1888, a young Piute Indian named Wovoka fell ill with a fever and had a dream. He said that the "Great Spirit" came to him and told him that an Indian god would soon appear. This god would return all the stolen lands to the Indians. All their dead friends would be brought back to life. The living Indians had only to sing and dance and pray. While the news spread among the superstitious Indians, an eclipse of the sun took place. They took this as a sign that Wovoka's prophecy was to be believed. Several other Indians fell into trances, all claiming that a great Indian triumph was on its way.

Sitting Bull now stepped forward to support this belief. In 1890, Indians across the West were dancing the Ghost Dance and wearing Ghost Dance shirts. These were decorated with magic symbols and the Indians thought they were bullet-proof.

The U.S. Government became alarmed by the unrest and ordered the capture of Sitting Bull. When they arrived at his cabin, agency officers found it surrounded by hostile supporters, who tried to prevent his arrest. In the fight that followed, Sitting Bull and one of the agency policemen were killed. The desperate resistance put up by the Indians of North America to retain ownership of their lands was now drawing rapidly to a close.

Angry Sioux began to assemble, and most of them truly believed that no harm could befall them as long as they wore their Ghost Dance shirts. Army detachments were sent out to put an end to the menace. Among them was the 7th Cavalry, Custer's old regiment.

The Indians were called upon to surrender, and many of them did. There was one band led by Chief Big Foot of the Minneconjou Sioux. He was old and suffering from pneumonia, but even so he ordered his followers to make for the Pine Ridge Agency, there to lay down their arms. Before they could reach the agency, the Sioux were overtaken by troopers of the 7th Cavalry under the command of Colonel James W. Forsyth.

The date was December 29, 1890, in the middle of winter. The ground was covered with snow and the weather was bitterly cold.

A ghost-shirt. The Indians believed that such shirts would protect them from the guns of the U.S. troopers. *(Photo: Bureau of American Ethnology.)*

The cavalry, reinforced with four Hotchkiss cannons, surrounded Big Foot's camp. Forsyth called upon the Indians to surrender their arms. Only two guns were produced. This enraged the colonel, and he ordered his soldiers to search the camp. When the Sioux protested, the soldiers began to knock down the tepees and push around the women and children. Reports differ as to what happened next, but it appears that an Indian shot a trooper. Instantly the Indians were mown down. When the fighting ended scarcely an Indian was still alive.

Sioux warriors, their old people, their women, their children, even their ponies, were gunned down in an orgy of slaughter. Some accounts stated that as many as 300 were shot down, while others reported that some 150 died. Of the troopers, about eight were killed. It is believed that several of these were slain accidentally by their comrades during the indiscriminate shooting.

This was the "battle" of Wounded Knee. Indian warriors in their pride would never again ride the war trail. Their gallant but futile effort to keep their hunting grounds was over.

TRIBES AND CUSTOMS

Apaches, Cheyennes, Sioux, Comanches, and Nez Perce were not the only tribes who fought to retain their hunting grounds. Others, too, are famous in Western history. Among them are the Blackfeet, the Crows, the Navajos, the Arapahos, the Shoshones, the Pawnees, and the Utes, after whom the state of Utah was named.

The many Indian tribes of North America rarely spoke the same language. Some tribes, such as the Sioux (their correct name is Dakota), were made up of a number of smaller tribes. For example, there were the Two Kettles, Sissetons, Oglalas, Tetons, Hunkpapas, Brulés, Santees, Yanktons, Minneconjous, Assiniboins, Midewakantons, and Sans Arcs. Their languages were similar. They dressed differently from other major tribes.

In truth, it would be impossible to state how many different tribes there were in America before the white man came. Many tribes have now died out. J. Fenimore Cooper's famous classic, *The Last of the Mohicans*, describes one such case.

The names of the tribes were often descriptive. Blackfeet were called that for one of two possible reasons. The first was that members of the tribe wore black moccasins. The other reason is that an enemy tribe had once carried out a raid, taken all their horses, and set fire to the prairie. When the

Blackfeet trudged through the smoke-blackened grass, it stained their moccasins. The Dakotas, the large tribe with many sub-tribes, means "allies." For many years the Hunkpapa Sioux had the right to camp at the head of any Sioux gathering. Hunkpapa means "Those Who Camp At The Entrance."

Different names, different clothes, and different languages were abundant. In one way, however, Indians all over North America won the reluctant admiration of the white people. They were, with very few exceptions, extremely brave. They were ready to die for their families, their homes, and their way of life.

The Plains Indians were often on the move because they depended on the buffalos. As buffalo herds moved across the prairies in search

of grass to eat, the Indians followed the herds.

Buffalo meat was cut into strips and then dried in the sun. Preserved in that way for a long time, the meat was eaten during the winter when food was difficult to find.

Moccasins, clothes, bedding, shields, tepees, and snowshoes were all made out of buffalo hides. Sinews were used as thread for sewing and also for bowstrings. Their domestic utensils, such as drinking cups and spoons, were fashioned out of the animals' bones. Glue was made out of buffalo hooves. It is easy to understand, therefore, why the wholesale slaughter of the herds by white hunters, who took only the meat to eat, drove so many Indians to the warpath.

The evening before Indians rode out to attack, they would gather for the war dance. Each warrior would dance around in a circle and sing. He would appeal to his own "medicine" for protection against harm and evil spirits. This "medicine" could be a sacred object or a good luck amulet. It might even be a tree. All hoped that the religious rites, that were carried out during the war dance, would ensure the defeat of their enemies.

The Indian prized his horse above all his other possessions. Without it, he could not hunt buffalo and he could not ride out to war. Horses were always tethered close to tepees at nightfall and guarded by sentries. During the night, a raid might be launched for the sole purpose of stealing a tribe's horses. Any captured horse thief would be put to death.

Until the coming of the white man, the Indians had never thought of the wheel. They used a litter when transporting their possessions from one camp to another. This litter was called a travois. Until the Spaniards brought horses to America, the travois was pulled by hand or by a dog.

Today many of the Indians' traditions and ways of life have disappeared. Busy highways and railroads now cross the prairies where the buffalo roamed and the Indian hunted. Ranchlands, fertile fields and farms dot the plains. The traditional life patterns of the Indians will never return in full.

Today, many tribes are working to regain their cultural heritage. Young children are taught the dances and arts of the old days. Indians on reservations are forming their own businesses and marketing to non-Indians. The land belonging to a reservation is recognized as a separate nation, regulated by its own laws. Some reservations even issue their own license plates.

No longer is the culture of Native Americans measured by European standards. Little by little, non-Indians are coming to appreciate and admire the art of American Indian tribes for its beauty and craftsmanship. So, too, is there a newfound admiration for the traditional way of Indian life, which took only what it needed from nature to survive.

He Dog, one of Crazy Horse's warriors. An Amulet, probably for good luck, hangs from his neck.

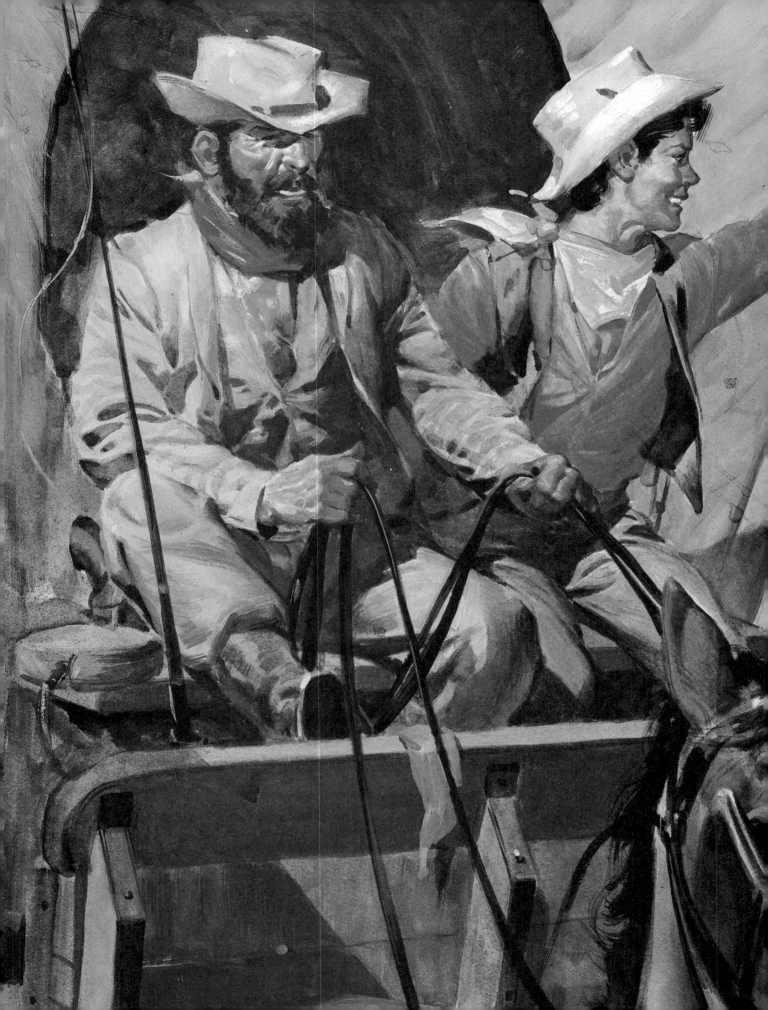

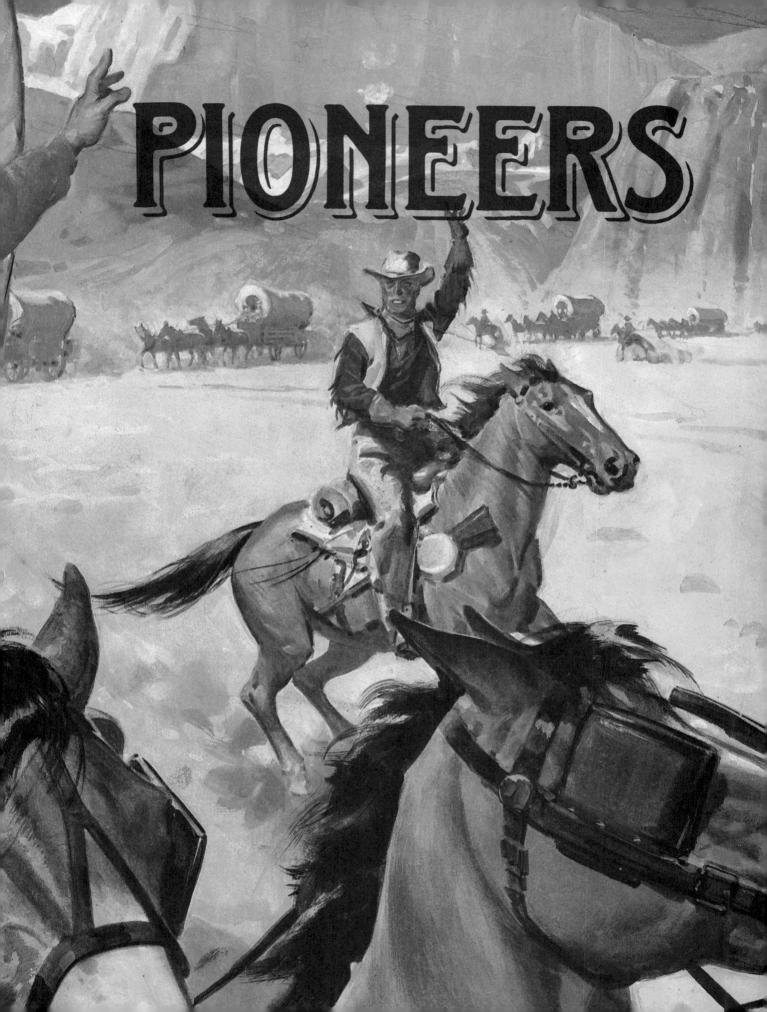

PIONEERS

PIONEERS

People came to the American West for different reasons. Some came looking for gold, and others were running away from trouble. But most people came because they wanted land.

In Europe and in the eastern section of North America, the good farming land was already being used. More and more people wanted new land on which to settle. They wanted somewhere to plant crops, raise stock and start families. They were looking for a new home.

About 150 years ago, thousands of people moved westwards from the Mississippi to settle in the vast western areas of North America. They tamed a wilderness and established farms and ranches, towns and cities. Without these settlers America would not be the country it is today.

The pioneers were not the first white men to travel in the West. Explorers and hunters had traveled across these wide-open spaces. They had met Indians and made maps of the country they crossed.

By 1840 some white men had traveled through the West. There were so few of them, however, that the West was virtually untouched. The pioneers would change all that.

PREPARING FOR THE JOURNEY

The pioneers moved west by several routes, or trails, and in several waves. The first important wave of settlers was that which moved along the Oregon Trail in 1843.

This was the largest of the early movements of settlers. In many ways the pioneers traveling the Oregon Trail were typical of many later settlers. It is worth telling their story in full.

The move to Oregon began in the 1830s. Many old mountain men and traders who worked for the Hudson's Bay Company, a large British fur company, retired in those years. Rather than move east, the retired men began farming in the Willamette Valley in Oregon Territory. The climate and land there were very similar to those in Europe. Farming was easy.

At about the same time Jason Lee, a minister, set up a mission in the Willamette Valley. In 1838, after some time in the valley, he traveled

East. He needed extra money to keep his mission going. Traveling through the eastern states, he gave lectures and collected money. Everywhere he went, Lee told people about the beautiful Willamette Valley and how easy it was to farm there.

The people of the East were excited. Many of them were looking for new land to farm. The land described by Jason Lee sounded ideal. Many people decided to move to Oregon to start a new life. In 1843, the first wagon train to arrive in Oregon complete with its wagons left Missouri. The guide was Marcus Whitman, and the immigrants numbered nearly 1,000. A wagon train with 100 people in tow had left Missouri in 1842, but the wagons were abandoned in the mountains.

The farmers reached Oregon safely and settled down to a life of farming. Other people in the East were encouraged by the success of this first wagon train. In 1844, hundreds of people decided to make the journey. Over the following years, several thousand people would follow the Oregon Trail across the plains. Their journey was never easy.

Most of the wagon trains started from Independence, a town in Missouri. Any farmer and his family wanting to travel to Oregon would come to Independence in April or May. Wagon trains always set off in spring so that they would reach Oregon before winter. For two months each year Independence became a hive of activity.

The journey was long and tiring. Each family knew it had to take everything that it might need on the long trail. Farmers had to take all the equipment they needed to start a farm. This was why the pioneers traveled in covered wagons. They carried all their farm equipment in the wagons. Many families also took several head of cattle or horses with them to start herds.

When the pioneers arrived in Independence they would get ready for the long journey ahead of them. First, they had to make sure that they had the right equipment. The most important equipment was the wagon which would carry the farmer, his family, and his tools. Most pioneers had a covered wagon like those seen in movies. There were, however, several dif-

An old engraving of Independence as it was in the early days of the pioneers.

ferent types of covered wagons.

In the early years many pioneers traveled in the same farm wagons that they had used at home. These were strong and could carry everything a

Wagon trains assembled in the town of Independence and prepared for the journey ahead.

pioneer wanted in his new home. Unfortunately, they were not designed for the long journey to Oregon. Many broke down on the way.

Later pioneers used different types of wagons built specially for the difficult journey across the West. The most familiar of these was the prairie schooner, or Conestoga wagon. It was about 25 feet long and had four wheels. A canvas covering swept upwards at either end. Pioneers tried to make sure that the bodies of the Conestogas were watertight. This would mean that they could float across rivers as if they were small boats.

A later type of wagon, used in Canada, was the Red River wagon. This was smaller than the Conestoga. The big advantage of the Red River wagon was that it did not use any metal in its construction. The wagon was made entirely of wood and could be easily repaired if it broke down. Like the Conestoga, the Red River also had a canvas cover. This kept everything inside dry when it rained and stopped the wind from blowing sand into the stores.

Before starting on their journey, the pioneers would make sure that the wagons were in perfect condition. Independence was the home of many blacksmiths. Everybody who visited the town during those pioneer years noticed there were far more blacksmiths than anywhere else. The blazing forges glowed late into the night and the clanging of hammers sounded around the clock.

The first pioneers used oxen to pull their wagons. Oxen moved only two miles each hour. However, they did not tire easily and were able to pull wagons all the way to Oregon.

Most wagons were pulled by either 6 or 8 oxen. When Oregon was reached the pioneers used the oxen to pull plows. Later pioneers, who did not need to travel such a long distance, used horses to pull their wagons. Horses could move faster and could be used for many different purposes once the journey was over.

Inside the wagon were the tools for working a farm. Wood for handles could be found in Oregon, so pioneers often carried only the metal parts of tools, such as axes, shovels and plows. Home utensils, such as saucepans, lanterns,

Above: **A typical family prepared and waiting for the long journey to begin.**

Right: **Cattle trudged alongside the wagons. Some would most likely be butchered for food when rations were short.**

bedding, and perhaps a few luxuries, were carried in the wagon. Buckets were hung underneath.

The pioneers also took other objects needed on the journey. These included spare parts for the wagons and food. The average wagon carried 150 pounds of flour and 15 pounds of coffee as well as other food. This would be enough to feed a family on the journey. Often, though, food ran out. The pioneers also took tents, because the wagons were so laden with equipment that they had to sleep outside.

Most of these tools and supplies could be bought in Independence. There were many shops in town which sold necessities to pioneers. During the years when it was the starting point for wagon trains, Independence was one of the busiest towns in America.

All pioneers carried guns. The early Oregon pioneers carried the single-shot pistols and rifles which were then available. Only later did pioneers carry revolvers and repeating rifles. These guns were not invented until later in the century.

THE FIRST FEW DAYS

With their wagon in top condition and enough supplies for the journey, the family's next step was finding a wagon train to join.

There were so many people in Independence that a family would have little trouble finding a wagon train. Generally speaking, all the families ready to leave at the same time would form a train.

There were many advantages to traveling in wagon trains. First of all, Indians and outlaws were unwilling to attack a large number of people.

Most of the benefits were more down to earth. If a family were traveling on its own, no one would be around to help them. If the wagon broke down, the family would be stuck in the middle of nowhere. In a large wagon train, however, there were lots of men to help fix a broken wagon. Perhaps one of them would be a blacksmith who could repair metal parts.

If a wagon could not be fixed, the pioneer family could divide their goods and stores into small amounts. These were then loaded into a number of other wagons. In this way the family would still arrive in Oregon with their equipment. Pioneers depended on each other a great deal during the long journey.

Once a wagon train was assembled, the pioneers would find a guide. Since none of the pioneers knew the way to Oregon, nor did any suspect what the journey would be like, each wagon train had to find an experienced guide.

Luckily there were plenty of men who did know the way. Mountain men and traders had been traveling in the West for a number of years. For these hardened frontier men, guiding a wagon train was an attractive idea. It was easier than trapping beaver or trading with Indians, and it paid well. Many tough frontiersmen could be found in Independence in the spring, each looking for a wagon train to guide.

It did not take long for a wagon train to find a guide. Fees were agreed to in advance. Usually the guide insisted that everyone in the train had to do exactly as they were told. Guides knew the dangers of the journey. Although an order from the guide might seem pointless to a pioneer, it was usually a sensible precaution. If one pioneer disobeyed the guide, the whole wagon train might be placed in danger. Most people were happy to do what the guide told them. Disagreements were rare.

When everything was ready, the wagon train set out from Independence. Most wagon trains left in May. There were very good reasons for this. First of all, the pioneers had to reach Oregon in time to build homes before winter arrived. On the other hand, the pioneers could not leave too early. They had to wait until the grass began to grow on the plains. Each wagon train had hundreds of oxen, cattle and horses

Many difficulties arose when a wide river was reached. At times the pulling of the wagon through the mud could take hours and at the River Platte many would-be pioneers turned back.

with it. There had to be enough grass on the plains to feed all these animals.

The first five days or so were fairly easy. The wagons rumbled across a gentle landscape which held few dangers. These were the 50 miles northwest to the Platte River. During these days, the guide got to know the pioneers in his train. The pioneers learned to accept the orders of their guide. It was a time when everybody became used to traveling together and to the routine of the march.

After 50 miles the pioneers reached the Platte River. This was a very wide, shallow river. One traveler noticed how much mud was in the Platte. He said it was "too thick to drink and too thin to plow."

Crossing the Platte was the first major event on the Oregon Trail. It could be dangerous. On the whole, the Platte was so shallow that the wagons could be driven across. However, there were hidden holes in the river bed. If a wagon fell into one of these, it might get stuck. Many hours could be spent trying to salvage a wagon. If a man fell into a hole or lost his footing, he might be swept away and drowned. Crossing the Platte was far from easy.

Once they had crossed the Platte, the pioneers were truly in wild country. It was the land of the Indians and the buffalos. It was at this point that the journey really began.

A photograph showing wagons crossing a river. Not all the rivers were as shallow as this one.

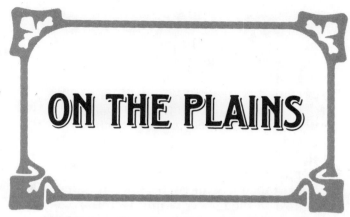

ON THE PLAINS

During the six weeks which it took to cross the plains, a daily routine was established. Everybody would wake up at dawn, about four o'clock in the morning. They would then cook breakfast and strike camp. This involved taking down any tents, collecting the tools used overnight, and packing everything into the wagons.

Meanwhile the animals had to be rounded up. The oxen and other livestock would have been turned loose to graze the previous evening. Though men would have been keeping an eye on them, some animals might have wandered a distance from the camp. The pioneers had to separate their own oxen from the rest. The men then hitched the oxen to the wagons. They made a last check to be sure that nothing had been left behind. Then they were ready.

About three hours after sunup, the wagon master would give the word to move. Wagons usually traveled in single file. Each wagon would follow in the path of the one before it.

This meant that only the front wagon had to worry about avoiding obstacles. The rest of the train just followed. Also, it was an easy task to persuade the oxen to follow other oxen.

The oxen pulled the wagons at about two miles per hour. Because the wagons were so loaded with stores and equipment, there was little room for people. Only the sick or immobile were allowed to ride in the wagon. Most pioneers walked beside the oxen. One member of the family would lead the oxen forwards. The others would help control the spare horses and the cattle. Some people might just stroll beside the wagon train.

Sometimes men who were good shots would ride separately from the wagon train. They would be looking for animals to hunt since pioneers did not take any meat with them. The only way to get meat was for hunters to go out and find it. Usually these hunters shot buffalo. They would butcher the animal on the spot and then carry the meat back to the wagon train.

Usually the wagon train would stop at noon for a short break. The pioneers would sit down for a rest. Perhaps they would eat a light meal. The animals would be allowed to graze. When the wagon master gave the word, the wagons would move forwards once again.

A few hours before dark, the wagon master would select a camp site and order the train to stop. If the wagon trains were to reach Oregon

in time, they had to travel twelve miles a day, sometimes less. Exactly how far they traveled each day depended largely on the terrain.

Setting up camp was a fairly complicated procedure. First of all, the wagons were arranged in a rough circle. This was a good defense against attack by Indians. The oxen were unhitched and allowed to graze on the rich plains grass. Then beds were made and cooking fires started.

Out on the plains there was no wood to burn. Instead, the pioneers burned lumps of what they called "prairie coal." In fact, these were dried buffalo droppings. Though not as good as wood, prairie coal could be made to burn fairly easily and produced a very good flame. Some of the stores brought in the wagons and meat shot by the hunters would be cooked for the evening meal.

Sometimes, if the pioneers were in a good mood, they might hold a dance. These dances did not last long into the night because everybody had to be on the move early the next morning.

Pioneers needed to provide entertainment and most evenings something was organized.

There was usually somebody in the wagon train who had brought a banjo or other musical instrument. There might be a good storyteller, or someone who had been to or come from Europe. These people would sit and talk while others gathered around to listen.

The plains across which the wagon trains traveled were the home of Indian tribes. Some of these tribes, such as the Sioux, Kiowa, and Comanche, have become famous. Many western films show wagon trains being attacked by Indians. Stories abound of hordes of whooping Indians galloping around circles of wagons, shooting arrows at the pioneers.

In truth this did not happen often. Pioneers were armed with rifles and pistols. Attacking a large group of men and women armed with guns would have been foolish. Indians usually did not bother. When the Indians did attack, however, they were a very real danger.

When the first wagon trains crossed the plains, the Indians were curious rather than hostile. The only white men the Indians had seen before the 1840s had been occasional trappers and traders. They had never seen so many whites at one time.

At night, wagons were arranged in a circle. This was a good defense against an attack by Indians.

Luckily, many of the wagon masters could speak Indian languages. They explained to the Indians that the pioneers did not want to cause trouble. All they wanted to do was to shoot a few buffalo for food and then move on. Once the Indians realized this, they left the wagon trains alone.

The early wagon trains ran into little trouble. Sometimes the Indians might try to steal horses or cattle. Occasionally, a fight might break out if a pioneer caught an Indian stealing or if an Indian felt he had been insulted. On the whole, the early wagon trains rarely fought the Indians. That trouble began later.

After several weeks the wagon trains reached Fort Laramie, or Fort John as it was called until 1849. There the wagon master allowed the pioneers to stop for a few days. The pioneers would rest and wash their clothes. If the wagons needed repairing, work could be carried out in the workshops of Fort Laramie. After this short break, the wagons headed towards the mountains.

THE MORMON EPIC

The Mormons are a religious sect which was founded in New York State in 1830. There were thousands of converts, and Mormon communities soon sprung up in many areas. Mormon beliefs angered many people. Under their leader, Brigham Young, they sought a new life in the West in 1846.

The wagon train that set out was the largest ever seen. It contained 12,000 people. It wintered in what is now Nebraska. Brigham Young rode ahead to find a place for his people to settle. Reaching a broad valley south of the Oregon Trail, Young said, "This is the place." The Mormons poured into the valley. Within years the wilderness had been transformed into fertile farmland.

The settlement centered around Salt Lake City, a town built by the Mormons in an amazingly short time. The whole of the Salt Lake Valley became an outpost of white civilization. It was hundreds of miles from the next settlement of whites. The Mormons had found what they were looking for: a country of their own.

Thousands of people heading for California stopped off at Salt Lake City. There, settlers in wagon trains could buy supplies and rest. Over the years, many settlers arrived who were not Mormons. Despite this, the area remained a stronghold of Mormonism. In 1896, the Mormon settlement became the state of Utah.

CROSSING THE MOUNTAINS

West of Fort Laramie, the Oregon Trail climbed to cross the Rockies at South Pass. In many ways the mountains were the most difficult part of the journey. The oxen had to drag the heavy wagons up steep hills for mile after mile. If the wagon train arrived late in the year, the pioneers had to cope with deep snow and ice.

The terrain made travel very difficult. Wagon trains were slow. The rocky ground broke many wheels and axles. If the wagons could not be fixed they had to be abandoned. Sometimes a wagon would run out of control and careen down a hill. When it crashed into the rocks at the bottom of a hill, the wagon

would be destroyed and many stores and tools would be lost. Many animals died on this stretch of the journey.

After crossing the South Pass, the wagon trains had a choice. They could either strike directly northwest or take a much longer route to the south. The shorter route had the disadvantage of being more difficult and without water holes. Pioneers usually only took this route if they were late. The longer route passed through better country. The two routes rejoined at Fort Hall on the Snake River.

The wagon trains then followed the Snake River for many miles. The Oregon Trail finally reached the Oregon River near Walla Walla. The official trail wound down the river to the Pacific Ocean. However, most pioneers never reached the sea. Instead, they turned south along the Willamette Valley or one of the other valleys.

Here the pioneers staked out their land claim. They finally unloaded their wagons for the last time and began their farms. Houses were quickly built to protect farmers during the winter. Land was cleared and made ready for planting in the spring. The long journey was over and the new land had been found!

Wagon trains rolled along the Oregon Trail for many years. In some places the passing of thousands of wagons cut such deep ruts that they can still be seen today. Many descendants of these pioneers still live in Oregon.

Pioneers, riding back to find some wagoners who had failed to keep up with the wagon train, would sometimes find their friends killed by Indians.

LATER SETTLERS

The American Civil War virtually halted all settlement in the West. While war raged in the eastern states, no one was eager to set out westwards. As soon as the war was over, however, the wagon trains began rolling again.

In some ways the post-war wagon trains were very similar to the earlier ones. In other ways they were very different. Physically, a wagon train of the 1860s and 1870s looked like those that had rumbled along the Oregon Trail in the 1840s. It was made up of Conestogas covered with white canvas. Everyone traveled in single file, and everyone obeyed the wagon master.

After the Civil War there were far more wagon trains. They moved across the plains in almost unbelievable numbers. Wagon train followed wagon train. More and more settlers arrived in the West.

The big rush of pioneers to the West was spurred by the Homestead Act of 1862. This act offered 160 acres of land in the West to anybody who went there and claimed it. All a man had to do was farm the land for five years and it was his. With the irresistible offer of free land, the settlers flooded westward.

New settlers did not stay on the Oregon Trail. They began to follow other trails to new areas of settlement. One of the most famous of these was the Santa Fe Trail. This route had been used since 1823 by traders and people traveling to Mexico. Now it was being used by wagon trains. Settlers moved along the Santa Fe Trail looking for good farmland that had never been farmed before.

All this angered the Plains Indian tribes. Instead of passing through, the wagon trains were stopping on Indian land. Settlers were beginning to farm on land previously inhabited by Indians. Even worse, from the point of view of the Indians, the settlers killed many more buffalo. Herds of these huge beasts were shot for food. Many more were killed to clear farmland. Professional buffalo hunters later slew thousands of the animals for their hides and tongues only. The Plains Indians relied on the buffalo. Slowly Indians began to realize the threat of the settlers.

Even before these mass emigrations, trouble had begun. In 1861, Cochise led the Apaches of Arizona on the warpath. In 1862, the Sioux attacked settlements on the edge of the plains at New Ulm, now in Minnesota. Hundreds of whites were killed before the Sioux were defeated about a year later.

From that time onward, warfare flared up and died down on the plains. In peace or war, the Indians remained a potential threat. Groups of young Indian warriors often carried out raids when they were meant to be at peace. To further complicate matters, a wagon train of settlers could not be expected to know which tribes were friendly and which were hostile. The settlers had to be on their guard with all Indians.

Wagons were formed into circles every night and lookouts stayed awake all night in case of attack. Still, Indians hesitated to attack wagon trains. They knew that the large numbers of armed men in a typical train would be able to beat off an Indian attack.

Stragglers were a different story. If a wagon fell behind the main train for some reason, it could be in terrible danger. When Indians saw an isolated target, they would pounce. A lone wagon stood little chance against an attack. Burned out wagons surrounded by arrow riddled bodies became depressingly familiar on the western plains. Men taking horses to water would be killed and their horses stolen.

These attacks were often more of a nuisance than a danger. Most wagon trains were safe from attack. The wagon master just had to make sure that his train took all possible precautions against attack.

In 1869, the transcontinental railroad was completed. Settlers had a new and better way of reaching the West. They could take the train deep into the plains. Only then would they take to the wagons and set off to find a piece of land.

By the end of the 1880s, the Indians were no longer a menace. The settlers could go where they wanted to in reasonable safety. In the search for new land, pioneers came westwards in large numbers and by many methods. Some

Rafts would have to be built at dangerous rivers and rapids.

A pioneer's wife prepares
a hasty meal.

traveled by railroad. Some came by wagon. Still others loaded their goods on rafts and traveled along rivers. This practice took place in the East and Midwest.

The years between the Civil War and the end of the century were the heyday of the pioneers. Even though pioneers could now reach their lands more quickly and safely, trouble was never far away. Starting a farm or ranch from scratch was no easy matter, as many pioneers learned the hard way.

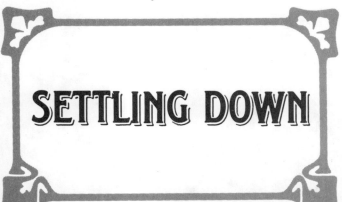

SETTLING DOWN

When the pioneers of the 1840s reached the end of the Oregon Trail, they found a land very much like that which they had left. The Willamette Valley was a pleasant land of forests and meadows.

After they arrived, the first thing the settlers did was find a place for their farms. Each man was allowed to claim 640 acres of land. Naturally he wanted to find the best 640 acres he could.

Each farm would need to include a section of river or stream. This would provide water for the farmer and his livestock. The stream might also be needed to irrigate the crops. The farmer would also want to include some meadowland, which would be useful grazing for his animals. He would also need an area of woodland to supply him with building materials and firewood. Luckily there was plenty of such land in the Willamette Valley and surrounding areas.

Of course, the local Indians had a great deal of contact with the white settlers. Some tribes were friendly, others were hostile. Whenever Indians were seen approaching, the farmer would arm himself. He could not afford to take chances.

Most settlers arrived in the early autumn. The first thing they did was to build a house. Often several families would join together to build the houses. Trees would be felled and logs shaped for building. Men from several families would join in to build houses in turn. In this way the buildings could be finished more quickly.

As settlements extended along the valleys, Indians became more and more hostile. Eventually, raids gave way to full-scale war. Log cabins were attacked by hostile Indians and settlers were killed or forced to flee. Eventually, the Indians were brought under control, not always by the most humane methods. Only then could the farmers of the far Northwest settle down to taming the landscape.

Farmers encountered many natural problems. Trees had to be cut down to clear land for crops, and marshy ground had to be drained. Grizzly bears and other wild animals had to be kept off the land. Despite these hardships, the settlers in the Oregon country managed very well. Within a few years the land was a patchwork of farms and settlements.

Farmers had to irrigate their fields with water from streams and rivers. This meant long periods of digging to create water channels. Along with the grain fields, there were gardens. Here the farmer's wife would raise vegetables for her family. These too needed constant work and water to produce a good crop.

Most settlers had some livestock. There might be a horse and a few head of cattle. These could be grazed on the open land near the farm or on rich meadowland within the farm.

Occasionally Indians would arrive at the farm. Usually they were friendly. Pilfering by Indians was not uncommon, and neither was horse stealing. Sometimes a full-scale war might erupt. Settlers would have to scurry for protection within the nearest fort. If they could not reach the fort in time, settlers faced death or hideous torture.

One of the biggest problems for the early plains settlers was the loneliness. The flat landscape stretched endlessly to the horizon. It could be miles to the next farm and a day's journey to anything which could be called a town. Apart from their own families, people could go for weeks without seeing anybody. If anything went wrong, there would be nobody to help.

The absence of people was too much for some settlers. They broke down and fled back East. Others thrived on the isolation and built up prosperous holdings.

Later pioneers who came to live on the plains had to cope with very different problems. Perhaps the most immediate problem for farmers on the plains was the lack of wood. How could farmers build houses without wood? The answer was the sod house.

Some trees grew along the banks of rivers on the plains. Timber cut from these trees was used to build a frame for a house. Then the farmer would set to work cutting pieces of turf, or sod, from the prairie. These were piled up against the wooden frame to form the walls and often the roof as well. These sod houses were surprisingly successful. They could be built quickly and cheaply. During the winter the sods kept in the heat of a stove. The summer

Log shacks could always be built at journey's end but the settlers had to be ready for the approach of hostile Indians.

sun beat down on sod roofs, which provided welcome shade.

With his house built, the settler could start farming. It might seem that the plains settler had an easier task than the settler in the Oregon country. He did not have to fell trees to clear land for crops. In fact, he faced a hard time getting started.

The soil on the plains was tough and difficult to plow. A farmer needed all his determination to turn his free 160 acres into a viable farm. Furthermore, the climate was a problem. The plains were much drier than the eastern lands where the pioneers had grown up. Rarely could fields of grain be planted and then expected to grow. In a wet year, wheat might grow easily. Most years, however, the wheat would sprout and then dry out and die before it was ripe.

As the numbers of people on the prairies in-

Once settled and their sod house built, the pioneers had to work hard on land that was not always very productive.

Grandfather and all his family pose for a photograph outside their sod house.

creased, new problems emerged. Before the farmers arrived on the western plains, the land had been taken over by the cowboys. With the plains swept clean of Indians and buffalo, the vast grasslands had been empty.

Enterprising ranchers moved in with herds of cattle. Within a short time hundreds of thousands of cattle were roaming the plains. Nobody owned the land on which the cattle grazed. Ranchers just turned their cattle loose on the open range and cowboys kept track of the cattle. The cattle of each ranch were branded to show who owned them.

When the first farmers began to arrive, the ranchers did not mind. If anything, they welcomed the farmers because it gave the cowboys people to talk to. If the farmer had a daughter, she might even marry a cowboy.

When the numbers of farmers increased, things changed. When a farmer arrived, he naturally wanted to settle on the best piece of land he could find. Except for the land of other settlers, none of the land belonged to anybody. The newcomer would choose a site on the

banks of a river and stake out his land.

After a time, the farms of the settlers could be found running along the banks of the rivers. This began to annoy the ranchers. They were used to their cattle roaming at will across the prairies. Disputes began to take place over water. Farmers were settling on the same river banks that cattle used as watering holes. When the cattle could no longer drink at the rivers, they began to die of thirst.

The farmers might have had a legal title to their patch of land, but the ranchers had got there first, and they had the guns to prove it. Several pioneers who refused to leave the farms were found shot dead. Others simply disappeared. At times the cowboys were the ones found dead. Such feuding occurred throughout the West. It cost the lives of many men and women but rarely erupted into major outbreaks of violence.

Perhaps the most famous of all range wars was the Johnson County War. By 1891 the ranchers of Johnson County, Wyoming, had had enough of farmers taking over prairie land. They hired 52 gunmen to blast the farmers off the range. In the violence which followed, the farmers defeated the gunmen.

Added to that, in 1886-87 a particularly savage winter killed thousands of cattle. Many ranchers went bankrupt. The plains now belonged to the farmers.

CIVILIZATION COMES TO THE PLAINS

Farmers and their families had always missed the civilized comforts of life in the East. When there were only a few pioneers earning a living on the soil, it was impossible to establish the civilization for which they longed. As numbers increased, however, so did the ambitions of the farmers.

The first sign of a maturing society was the appearance of towns. These towns could be strange places. Sometimes they were little more than a collection of shacks. Farmers from the surrounding prairie would come to town to meet and talk. There would normally be a store where farmers would buy supplies and equipment, and a saloon where they could meet for a drink and catch up on the latest news. Perhaps there would also be a blacksmith to help repair metal tools.

As railroads spread across the West, a new kind of town began to spring up. It was the railroad town. In many cases railroad towns were similar to the earlier shack towns. In addition to the other stores, they had a railroad station, and often a telegraph office. This meant that they were in contact with the outside world. Goods and equipment could be shipped in by train. The crops raised by the farmers could be sold to the railroad. A town with a railroad was always a larger and richer place than one without a railroad.

As more and more farmers moved on to the prairies, towns grew larger. They came to be the centers for a countryside full of farmers. Towns might now number a few hundred people. There would be several stores. Many services were available: blacksmiths, launderettes, hotels, saloons, and schools.

Almost as soon as there were enough children in an area, a school would appear. The schools were fairly primitive by modern standards. Children learned reading, writing, and arithmetic, but little else. As soon as children were old enough to help on farms, they left school.

One man who was the son of a pioneer in South Dakota wrote about his school days. He remembered that each day he and his brother started for school. If any cattle were on the range between the farm and town, the boys turned back. This was because the cattle were half wild and very dangerous.

Another building likely to be found in these early towns was a church. The communities of farmers felt a need of religion in their lonely lives. When a pastor arrived, the whole community would pitch in to build a church. Everyone would help by bringing building materials or by spending time working on the building. These churches might be of one particular denomination, or of no denomination at all. Churches were a central part of any town and often formed the center of society.

Very different from the churches were the saloons. Some of these were wild drinking places where brawls were common. Many

more were simple, peaceful places where a farmer could meet his friends for a quiet drink. A few saloons were very grand. These were usually found in the larger towns. These saloons had stages and engaged actors and actresses to entertain the customers.

Throughout the closing years of the last century, the West saw a long parade of impressive stars. World famous singers and actors traveled by train to many towns in the West. Some theatrical companies even came from Europe to tour the West. Such visits may have been rare, but they provided great excitement in the farming communities.

The law found its first place in these towns. During the early days of the pioneers, law came from the barrel of a gun. It was only after farmers settled in large numbers that law and order could be enforced. Towns would elect sheriffs to enforce the law. Often these sheriffs were little better than the men they tried to keep in order.

Sometimes towns faced with a serious problem would deliberately hire a killer as sheriff. Only a hired gun would dare to try to impose law and order on a dangerous town. Such men as these created order in a town, often by shooting anybody who crossed them.

Usually, of course, sheriffs were respectable men. Their duties included locking up drunks and keeping an eye on young troublemakers. Only rarely did sheriffs have to tackle anything more dangerous.

The progress of the pioneer settlement from wagon train to peaceful town was a long one. Often the original pioneers were dead by the time a town came into existence. The part played by the pioneers was vital to America. They tamed a wilderness and made it a rich and fertile land. With sheer determination and courage these men and women carved a nation out of a wild country. The covered wagons and hard-working farmers have taken a rightful place in American history.

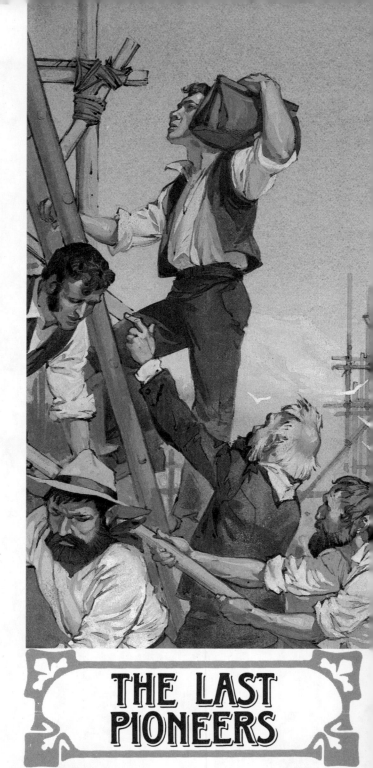

THE LAST PIONEERS

By 1890 the age of the pioneer seemed to be over. Only one more episode remained to be played. All of the West was taken up by farmers, ranchers or Indian reservations.

The largest reservation was that which covered the modern state of Oklahoma. The land was occupied by the tribes of the Cherokees, Creeks, Choctaws, Chicasaws and Seminoles. At the start of 1889, the tribes announced that they were willing to sell large

Everyone from far and wide would pitch in to help with the building of a church.

A street in Guthrie, a town which was settled in two and built in four days. The sheriff is ready to greet all newcomers.

areas of their reservation. The government bought nearly two million acres of land and prepared to open it up for settlement.

The government decided that the lands would be opened to pioneers at noon on April 22. Nobody would be allowed into the land before that time. Once the signal for settlement was given, people would be free to stake any piece of land they wanted. Each man would be able to claim 160 acres.

Word soon got around that there was free

This photograph is of the actual Oklahoma landrush in April, 1890.

land available. As April 22 approached, thousands of people arrived in Arkansas City, the official starting line for pioneers wishing to claim land. On April 19, the covered wagons rumbled forward towards unclaimed land. They moved out of Arkansas City towards the new lands.

Army scouts rode through the lands to be opened for settlement. They made sure that nobody had cheated and tried to claim land before April 22.

On the morning of April 22, soldiers under the command of Captain Hays of the 5th Cavalry were strung out along the border of the new lands. In front of them were thousands of people, all eager to claim farms. The soldiers were under orders to stop anybody passing them until Captain Hays signaled that it was noon.

The settlers had come from all over America. Some were in covered wagons. Others were mounted on fast horses, determined to be the first to the best land. A few were on foot, too poor to afford even a horse.

All through the morning the settlers waited while tension mounted. At a few minutes to noon Captain Hays raised his hand in the air. Thousands of eyes were fixed on his arm. A deathly hush fell over the waiting crowds.

Suddenly Captain Hays dropped his hand. A great cheer went up from the settlers. They charged forwards, each man traveling as fast as he could. Within a single day, all the land had been claimed. Guthrie and Oklahoma City had been founded and the citizens had set up local government.

In 1893, another huge land rush took place. It was the end of an era for the pioneers of the West. Ever since the first wagons had creaked over the Oregon Trail in the 1840s there had been free land. Anybody who was adventurous enough to claim a farm could have one free.

Thousands of people had moved westward to look for a better life. They had faced incredible dangers. Settlers had traveled over vast distances. They carved farms out of a wilderness. Towns sprang up from nothing.

Now it was all over. There was no new land to settle. There were no free farms to claim. The age of the pioneers was over.

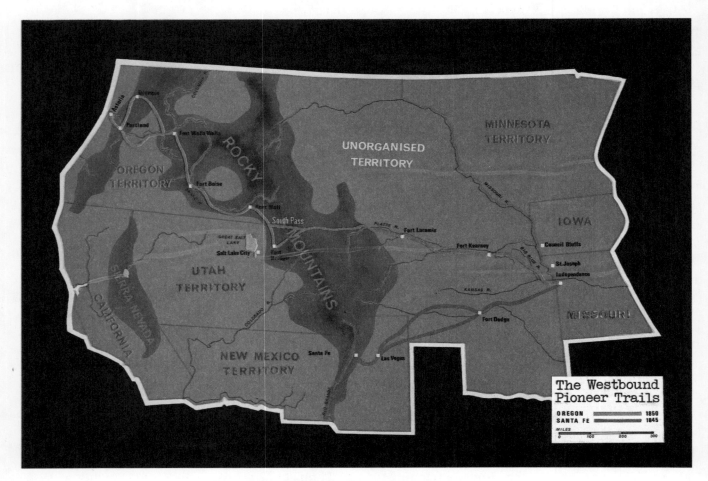

The Westbound
Pioneer Trails

OREGON ▭▭▭▭ 1850
SANTA FE ▭▭▭▭ 1845
MILES
0   100   200   300

PREPARATION

True grit! That is what anyone who wanted to be a settler in the untamed West had to have. True grit, for there would be months ahead when only the bravest of the brave could possibly hope to win through and reach their goal.

Those hardy pioneers who set out on the westward trails towards the rich and fertile lands knew and understood this. Imagine how brave they were, these sons and daughters of early America, and just think how the odds were stacked against their ever arriving at journey's end!

The pioneers had to cross a continent in wagons that they prayed would withstand the hardships of lumbering across endless miles of rocky ground. How they must have hoped that their horses and oxen would not fall ill or their wagons break down as they plodded across the vast prairies and toiled over high, snow-capped mountains.

How much warm clothing would they have to take? How many pairs of stout boots? How much food for the first few weeks before their hunters and scouts could shoot game to satisfy their hunger? What medical supplies? What guns? How much ammunition? All these questions and many more had to be answered, since they could make all the difference between life and death.

Apart from all the perils of wild, savage lands and harsh weather conditions, there were other dangers. These pioneers were, for the most part, honest, hard-working people who had saved the money they would need when they reached their "promised land." This hard-won cash was probably locked away in strong-boxes and stowed aboard the wagons, not to be opened until they were ready to settle down. This fact was known to the many bandit gangs that lined the trails, and the settlers had to be on constant watch for these killers. Their attacks were sudden and merciless.

Then, too, there were always the savage tribes of Indians — the Comanches, the Cheyennes, the Blackfeet and the Sioux. Sometimes these warriors could be bought off with a few trinkets or a horse or two. Even then they could not be trusted to let the wagons pass unhindered. The next day, at dawn, those same Indians, now painted for war, might well be creeping up unseen, bent on slaying every pioneer and making off with their wagons and cattle. From the Indians' point of view, they were defending their lands.

Even when the weary travelers had arrived at their destinations, they could be faced with bitter disappointment. For instance, several riders who took part in the Oklahoma land rush of April 22, 1889, were astonished to find that someone else had arrived there first. How had this happened? Several of those late arrivals knew that they had been ahead of the other riders. How could the plots they hoped for have already been staked out? Yet here were scowling men who, with guns ready, showed no sign of having ridden for miles and whose fresh horses were nibbling grass nearby.

The simple answer was that these gunmen were what were then called "sooners." They sneaked in the night before, having successfully avoided the army sentries posted to guard against such crooked tricks. The sooners had planted their stakes. They were more than willing to prove their ownership of a particular piece of ground with the aid of their guns. In those hard days, possession was often worth more than nine-tenths of the law.

Looking back now, one wonders why it was that so many thousands of settlers set out in the first place. One reason was their dauntless spirit of high adventure, their courage to reach out and grasp the danger to improve their station in life. This spirit has always been a great part of the American nation.

Rough and tough were the lives of those early pioneers. Few people now could be tempted away from their mothers, their fathers, their comfortable homes, their cars, and their television sets, to set out on such dangerous adventures. Somehow, though, it seems sad that today nowhere in the world and never again can there be such another time or such opportunities offered to the young and brave in heart.

A Conestoga wagon

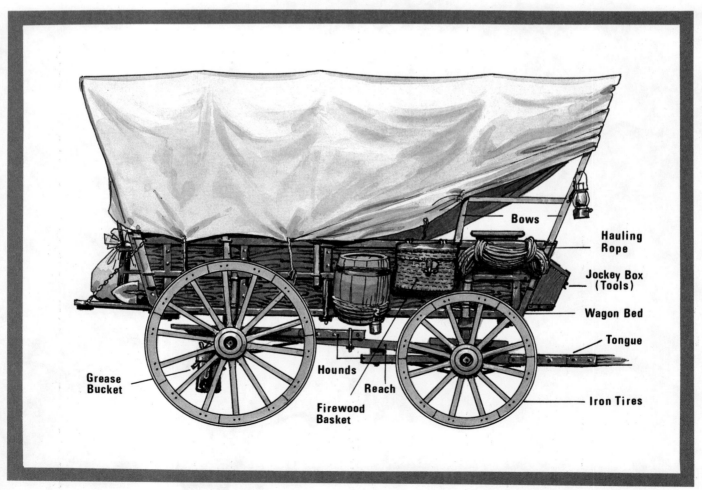

COWBOYS

COWBOYS

Of all the heroes of the American past, perhaps none is as romantic or as exciting as the cowboy. He rode tall in the saddle and long in the stirrup. He knew right from wrong. He was quick to fight for justice and stuck to a friend come what may.

It is strange that the cowboy has come down to us only as an image. Wyatt Earp is thought of as the typical marshal, Jesse James as the most notorious bandit, and Custer as the best known Western soldier. There is no one cowboy, though, who stands out from the rest.

This is probably just as the cowboys would have wanted it.

They did not chase fame. The average cowboy was content to do his work well and draw his pay. Sometimes this work was tough and lonely; sometimes it was easy. On occasions it was dull and tedious, and every now and then it was nerve-racking. Whatever job he was doing, the cowboy was working with cattle and with horses.

Our image of the cowboy is of a man at one with his horse and his cattle. What is the real truth behind the image? What were cowboys really like? As with many subjects, the truth about the cowboy is even more interesting than the image.

THE COMING OF THE CATTLE

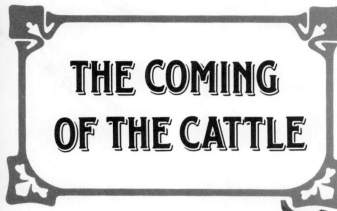

Coronado and his intrepid followers marched north to Arizona with a herd of nearly 500 head of cattle.

Cattle are not native to North America. Before the white man came to North America, millions of buffalo and deer roamed the plains and forests, but there were no cattle.

The Spanish brought the first cattle to the plains, which were destined to become the greatest cattle range the world has ever seen. The very first of these animals arrived with Gregorio de Villalobos on the banks of the Panuco River in Mexico. The year was 1521. Soon hundreds of other cattle had arrived, and Mexico had a thriving beef industry.

As the Spanish conquistadores spread northward, they took their cattle with them. Francisco de Coronado marched north in 1540 with a herd of nearly 500 head. They traveled at least as far north as what is today the state of Arizona. Later explorers following Coronado found large numbers of wild cattle. These were the descendants of cattle turned loose by the early explorers.

Settlers continued to bring more cattle with them, until eventually Spanish cattle were grazing far into Texas. The Spanish settlers built up a very successful cattle industry in northern Mexico. They raised cattle for their hides and their meat.

Many of the objects later to be part of cowboy culture originated with the Spanish, who at this time ruled Mexico. It was the Spanish who first had ranchos, or cattle ranches. The high-pommelled cowboy saddle is copied from the saddles of conquistadores. The Spanish settlers also introduced the broad brimmed

The Texas cowboys could skillfully rope a longhorn steer at the gallop.

This is a genuine longhorn steer, menacing and dangerous as it prepares to charge. (Photo: Denver Public Library. Western History Dept.)

hat, which was ideal for conditions on the plains. High-heeled boots, needed to brace a cowboy in his saddle, and jangling spurs were also adopted from the Spanish. Chaps, worn on the legs to protect against sharp thorns, were a Spanish invention. Even the places where a cowboy worked, his ranch and corral, were patterned after those on the Spanish ranchos.

But the cowboy was not a totally Spanish creation. The way Texans borrowed Spanish ideas and changed them to fit their own needs created the true cowboy. For instance, the Spanish used a long pole called a desjarretadera. This had a large curved blade mounted at one end. It was used to hamstring cattle before slaughter. The Spanish also used long poles to place loops of rope over the heads of cattle. The Texas cowboy used the same rope, or lariat, but he learned to throw it with great skill. The cruel desjarretadera was no longer needed.

Perhaps the greatest contribution the Spanish brought to North America was the longhorn cow. This breed was ideal for the tough conditions in America. They were descended from the Andalusian cattle of the Arabs and were bred for life on the dry plains of Spain. The longhorns took to life in North America with relish. They were tough and strong enough to look after themselves on the bleak plains. Longhorns were big cattle with huge horns, which often reached six feet from tip to tip. They could fight off wolves and even pumas. All the longhorn needed to thrive was grass and water.

The disadvantage of these cattle was that they were half wild. Longhorns could not be pastured and handled like tamer breeds of cattle. They would unpredictably turn and attack a man with their fearsome horns. But the early cowboys did not have much choice. If a man wanted cattle that would survive on the plains, he had to have longhorns.

These were some of the legacies left behind by the Spanish. By the mid 1800s, the growing power of the United States had driven the Spanish out of Texas and the Southwest.

THE BONANZA IN BEEF

A noonday halt to water the cattle and horses. (Photo: Kansas State Historical Society. Topeka).

During the Civil War many Texans left their state to join in the fighting. Remaining on the land were thousands of cattle. When the fighting was over, the survivors went home to Texas. There they found that their cattle had run wild. Now there were millions of longhorns wandering around the grasslands of Texas.

Although the Texans had vast numbers of cattle, no one in the West wanted to buy them. These Texans were called cow-poor. They had a potential fortune but no money.

The big cities of the East, however, were eager to eat Texas beef. The solution to the Texans' problem was to drive their cattle to the Eastern cities. There were no cars or trucks at that time. The only way to move cattle from one place to another was to make them walk.

Of course, a cattle drive was not so simple. In 1866, when the first big herds set out, the country was still in turmoil. Several herds were attacked by outlaws. The cowboys were shot and their cattle stolen. In other places farmers stopped the cattle drives. The farmers were afraid that the Texas cattle were bringing disease with them. In fact, of the thousands of cattle that set out from Texas in 1866, very few reached a market.

Then Joseph McCoy came on the scene. McCoy, a cattle dealer from Chicago, had an idea. He believed that if a railroad could be built west into Kansas, the Texas cattle could be loaded on rail cars and taken East. After being turned down by several railroad companies, McCoy talked the Hannibal and St. Jo company into backing his idea.

McCoy chose the town of Abilene in Kansas as a destination. The town had plenty of good grass around it on which the cattle could graze. It was outside the reach of angry farmers. Most important of all, Abilene had a railroad. In the summer of 1867 McCoy started building stock pens and railroad sidings. He also sent a rider south to tell the Texas cattlemen what was happening in Abilene.

The first herd arrived before McCoy had even finished the pens. Soon thousands of cattle were congregating in Abilene. The huge herds of cattle could now be taken to market much more easily. This was the beginning of the boom in cattle that took place during the following twenty years.

Cattle ranching soon spread far and wide as cowboys drove herds onto any piece of land that had grass. In a few years, ranches sprang up all across the plains from the Rio Grande to beyond the Canadian border. The cowboy soon became the most important person on the plains.

THE COWBOY AND HIS HORSE

For twenty years the cowboy was the undisputed master of the plains. He rode, straightlegged in the saddle, across the long, empty miles. The great open spaces were his home. His way of life depended on his horse and his equipment, all of which was superbly adapted to the harsh conditions of the range.

The cow pony was descended from the horses brought to America by the Spanish. Some of these had run wild. Only the fittest and toughest survived a wild life on the plains. These eventually created the breed called mustang, the wild horse of the plains. These were the horses that were captured and broken to be cow ponies.

The ponies had a stubborn streak of independence, and there was no time for a long taming process. Cowboys tamed their mustangs by simply putting a saddle and a harness on them. The cowboy then mounted. The mustang at once tried to buck the man off. The cowboy just hung on until the horse gave up trying to dislodge the man. Many times the horse won the first round, flinging the cowboy into the dust. All the cowboy could do was climb back into the saddle and try again.

The expert horse breaker got to know all the tricks a mustang might try. There was the crow hop, the sun fish and the rainbow, all of them

Taming a wild mustang was a tough and dangerous job. Only top class riders could hope to survive.

bone-jarring leaps and twists made by the horse to throw the rider. This method of breaking horses was the origin of the exciting bucking bronco events at modern rodeos.

Once broken, the horse would be slowly trained in the skills of a cow pony. These skills were many and varied. A good cow pony was a highly prized possession. Though each cowboy might own his own horse, the working horses were provided by the ranch. Cowboys would ride different horses depending on which job they were going to do. Most ranches would have about six horses for each cowboy.

A newly broken horse would be used for the simple jobs that did not need much skill. These jobs would include riding line, or patrolling the more isolated parts of the ranch, and looking for strays. A horse that was a good swimmer was used when cattle had to be pushed across rivers. Longhorns did not like to swim. If they had horses to follow, they were more likely to cross quietly. Night horses were able to find their way in the dark without stumbling or treading in holes.

The most highly prized and most rigorously trained of all cow ponies were the roping and the cutting horses. Roping horses were used to catch individual cows, calves, or steers. Longhorns were dangerous animals and could easily kill a man on foot. The cowboy had to rope cattle from horseback. The roping horse was trained to respond to the slightest touch by the rider while he was busy with his rope. When the cowboy had roped a cow, he would wrap the rope swiftly around the saddle pommel. At this point the cow pony had to brace itself for the shock. The cow would usually try to break away. Only the strongest roping horse could hold a full grown longhorn when it wanted to escape.

Cutting horses were the most valuable of all the cow ponies. These animals were tough and agile. Cowboys used cutting horses when a particular cow had to be cut out, or separated, from her herd. The cowboy had to position his horse between a particular cow and the rest of the herd. The longhorn would try to get back to the herd. Whichever way the cow turned, the cowboy had to be there first to block the way back to the herd. Good cutting horses seemed to have an instinct for this work. They could turn around sharply and move from a standstill to a full gallop with a bound. It is little wonder that cowboys prized these horses so highly.

THE MAN AND HIS GEAR

The life of a cowboy was hard and tough. Very often his life depended on the equipment he carried on his horse. Everything a cowboy wore or used had to be practical and durable. The cowboy also had to

This photograph of an old-time cowboy illustrates clearly the typical Western saddle. (*Photo: D. Butcher Collection, Nebraska State Historical Society*).

be able to carry it all on his horse.

The saddle bore the weight of all this equipment. Though there were various styles of cowboy saddles, they all conformed to a set pattern. The saddles were built around a wooden frame. A strong iron core was fitted to the pommel to take the strain of roping cattle. The saddle around the pommel was often raised up to fit snugly around the rider. For the same reason, the cantle was raised high behind the seat of the saddle. This basic frame was covered by layers of tough leather. Cowboys found this shaped saddle useful in rough country or when working cattle. The shape helped the rider stay firmly in the saddle.

The saddle was held on the horse by two girths that were cinched, or tied, into place. This unusual arrangement was needed because roping a steer put tremendous strains on a saddle. No single girth or buckle could withstand the pressure.

Cowboys' boots had narrow toes to slip easily into stirrups and high heels which kept the spurs clear of the ground.

Spreading out from the saddle was the skirt, a square of leather, which gave the rider a better grip with his knees. Attached to the skirt were several leather thongs. These were used to tie objects to the saddle. These might be blanket rolls, yellow slickers (water-proofs), rifles, or a host of other equipment. To stay in his saddle, the cowboy depended on his stirrups. Cowboy stirrups were much larger than those used for other kinds of riding. The cowboy had to be able to leap in and out of the saddle quickly and easily.

All in all, a saddle might weigh over forty pounds. It was probably the only expensive thing most cowboys would own. A good saddle might cost a cowboy about four months' wages.

A cowboy's clothes were just as practical as his saddle. From head to toe the cowboy was dressed in clothes superbly fitted to his way of life.

The famous cowboy boots were a wholly American invention. The essential ingredients of narrow toes, high heels, and long legs only came together in 1878 when a cowboy persuaded a Texan boot maker to turn out a pair of

boots to order. The high heels served two purposes. They allowed the cowboy to brace himself in the stirrups. They also kept the large spurs attached to the back of the boots clear of the ground when the cowboy was walking.

Spurs were used both to help a rider hang on to a horse and to make the horse go faster. The reason for the large spurs was that the horses were small and the men rode with their legs straight. If the spurs had been smaller, a cowboy would have had difficulty reaching the horse's body. The large spurs also jingled pleasantly and cowboys sometimes wore fairly showy creations.

In the bitterly cold winters of the northern states, the cowboys needed chaps of goat's hair to keep them warm.

On his legs the cowboy often wore the most striking feature of his working clothes, chaps. Originally designed by the Mexicans as cha-parejos, chaps protected a cowboy's legs in scrub and cactus. The Spanish word for a dense thicket of low, thorny shrubs is chaparro; in English chaparral means the same thing. The tough leather of the chaps prevented the thorns and prickles from tearing trousers and cutting legs.

In Arizona the chaps were famous for being huge and wide so that they protected the flanks of the horse almost as much as the legs of the rider. Elsewhere the chaps were narrower, almost hugging the legs. In the northern plains of Wyoming and Montana, a different style emerged. The cold winters that struck these states meant that the cowboys had to keep as warm as possible. They often covered the fronts of their chaps with goat hair. This gave them a shaggy look.

Essential to a cowboy's work were his gloves. So much of his time was spent working with ropes and reins that a cowboy's hands would have been rubbed raw within a few days. The gloves protected his hands. They were made of tough buckskin, but even so it was surprising how quickly a cowboy could wear them out.

The bandanna a cowboy wore wrapped around his neck was useful for many purposes. The cowboy could mop sweat from his eyes with his bandanna or tie up a wound. It protected the back of his neck from the hot sun and prevented possible sunstroke. He also wore it to cover his nose and mouth when winds whipped up the sand and dust. Despite this, many cowboys did not wear bandannas, and they were not as common as some people think.

The cowboy hat is perhaps the most famous item of Western clothing. When cattle ranching began cowboys were happy with almost anything that came to hand. The purpose of a hat was to protect the wearer from the weather. Soon, however, the scorching Texas sun caused the cowboys in that state to copy the wide-brimmed hats of the Mexicans. As usual, the Texans were not content with things as they were and improved the hat by giving it a high crown and a floppy brim. In the 1870s the round-crowned hat of hatter J.B. Stetson became increasingly popular. During the following decade the "Montana Pinch" style became popular on the northern plains.

The rifle and the handgun were tools of the trade for the cowboys who were hard workers, not hardened killers.

Cowboy hats may have changed over the years, but all cowboy hats have wide brims and high crowns. The wide brim is good for keeping both the sun and the rain away from the cowboy. During the cold winter months, the brim could be tied down to form a pair of ear muffs. The high crown was often used to hold water from which either man or horse could drink. The hats came in for a lot of hard wear. Cowboys have always been willing to pay a high price for a hat. A good one lasts for years.

Other items were of vital importance to a cowboy. Of these, the most famous are probably the rope and the gun.

The gun was essential to the cowboy, but he was not a hardened gunfighter as some movies suggest. In fact, the gun was a tool that a cowboy had to carry. He never knew when he might run into a puma or a wolf. Encounters with human enemies were much more rare.

A cowboy wore his gun when he was riding the range, particularly if he was near Indian Territory, simply because of the dangers he might encounter. He would also carry a gun when driving cattle. If the cattle stampeded, the cowboy might have to shoot a steer to save himself from being gored. On the other hand, when he was branding calves or working around the ranch, he did not need to wear a gun. Guns were heavy and could get in the way. At the same time, if a cowboy wanted to look his best he put on a gun. He might be taking a trip to town or calling on a lady. The gun was thought to be part of the proper dress for a cowboy.

The gun most often seen, of course, was the Colt revolver. Other makes were used by cowboys, but the Colt was the favorite. It weighed over two pounds, and its barrel was eight inches long. It was not a particularly good weapon for gunfights, nor was it very accurate. If a cowboy shot at anything further than 75 feet away, he was almost certain to miss. The Colt was designed for fast, effective shooting at close range. For this it was perfect.

For hunting or long-range shooting, cowboys used rifles. At the height of the cattle years, the most popular rifle was the Winchester. Most cowboys carried a rifle strapped to their saddles. These guns were certainly far more effective at long range than any pistol. Because they were much heavier and clumsier than a Colt, they were rarely used for close, fast shooting.

A cowboy's rope was essential for his work with cattle. Longhorns were famous for their bad tempers. A steer was likely to attack a man who came too close. The only way around this

Roundup time in the West.

A midday camp fire meal during the roundup. (*Photo: Wyoming State Archives and Historical Society*).

was to catch it with a rope and make sure that it was incapable of doing any harm.

The earliest ropes were made of rawhide and were about 35 feet long. Cowboys called these ropes lariats, from the Spanish words la reata, which mean "the rope." Rawhide lariats were easy to throw, but if a single string broke, the whole lariat was useless. In Texas, ropes made of maguey, a cactus-like plant, were popular. Maguey ropes were tough and threw well. They were often up to 75 feet long. They were of little use outside Texas, though, because they could not be used in wet weather.

The most popular lariat of all was made from hemp from the Philippines. These ropes were used throughout the West. They may not have thrown as well as rawhide or maguey lariats, but hemp ropes were strong and reliable in all kinds of weather.

THE YEAR ON THE RANCH

The most exciting and demanding time of year on any ranch was the spring roundup. This was the time when the cattle were brought in from the range to be counted and branded. After the long, cold months of winter, the cowboys could once again gallop across the plains. It was a welcome relief for the cowboys.

During the years immediately after the Civil War, roundups were still somewhat disorganized. They were called cow hunts, which describes them perfectly. The cowboys rode off onto the grasslands and into the scrub to hunt down any cattle they could find.

In the early days, many thousands of wild cattle roamed the plains. The first man to catch a steer or a cow and place his brand on it became the owner. An energetic cowboy could come back from a cow hunt as the proud owner of a sizable herd.

These unbranded cattle became known as mavericks. In 1847, Colonel Samuel Maverick acquired a herd of cattle in Texas. He decided not to brand them, since the cattle on all the neighboring ranches were branded. Unbranded cattle would be recognized as his, he reasoned. As the story is told, each time he heard of an unbranded cow or steer, he tried to claim it. The term maverick came to be used for any unbranded cattle.

By the mid-1870s most mavericks had been claimed. The old cow hunts turned into highly organized roundups. Every large ranch had a foreman and many cowboys, while a smaller ranch was run by the owner. He was also the only cowboy. Whatever their size, all ranches grazed their cattle on the open range. During the months of grazing, everyone's cattle mixed together.

Every year the longhorns had to be gathered together and divided up according to ownership. The new-born calves belonged to the same ranch as their mothers and needed to be marked with that brand. Branding was important because it defined ownership, and changing a brand was a serious crime.

At first, roundups were organized by the local ranchers. Later, they were controlled by local cattlemen's associations. A date and place were arranged for the start of the roundup. Cowboys from every ranch in the district arrived at the designated place. When the word was given, the roundup began.

The cowboys rode out in all directions looking for cattle. They might find some in small herds or alone. The cattle might be grazing or browsing in thickets. Wherever they were found, the cowboys would gather them together in small herds or bunches. Once gathered, the cattle would be driven back to the starting point.

While some cowboys were riding off in search of cattle, others built fires and started heating up the branding irons. They were ready to start branding as soon as the cowboys drove in cattle.

The herds were stopped some distance from the branding fires. Then the cowboys would start their rope work. The main task was to catch the calves for branding. The cowboys worked in pairs, one riding a cutting pony and the other a roping horse. The cutter would push his horse into the herd to separate a calf from the rest of the cattle. Once the cutter had

Cowboys often fought for their lives while protecting cattle from bands of outlaw rustlers and raiding Indians.

the calf away from the herd, the roper would move in.

Swinging his lariat, the roper chased and caught the calf. Ropers used different techniques to catch cattle. The "heeling catch" was used to drop the loop of the lariat just in front of the hind legs of a steer. When pulled tight, the rope tripped the animal and threw it to the ground. A "forefooting slip" caught an animal by its front legs, with a similar tripping effect.

Once the calf was roped, it was dragged to the branding fire. The roper would shout out the brand seen on the calf's mother. The branders would select the correct iron from the fire. Then they would brand the calf.

As well as branding all the calves, roundups served other purposes. One of the most important of these was cutting out the cattle to be sold. These cattle were usually about four years old. At this age the longhorns were fully grown, but their meat had not yet become too tough to eat. When all these cattle had been cut out from the main herd, they were herded together, ready to be taken to market. This

market might be many hundreds of miles away. Cowboys would have to drive the cattle for many weeks. The best and fittest cowboys were chosen for this task.

As the trail herds set off for market, the other cowboys returned to the ranch. These ranches came in many shapes and sizes. Some were plush, others were just a collection of sheds. Most ranches had the same problem: a lack of building materials. There were few trees on the plains, so there was little wood to build a house.

The early ranches were very simple. Some consisted of just a couple of dugouts. These buildings were nothing more than holes dug into the side of a hill. A roof was put over the hole and a door built at one end. Dugouts were dirty and leaked whenever it rained. But if a fire was built properly, a dugout was very warm in the winter.

Only slightly better than dugouts were sod houses. As their name suggests, sod houses were built out of sods of turf. These were cut from the prairie grass and shaped into large squares. The sods were piled on top of one another to form the walls of the house. The roof was built of wooden rafters, which were covered with even more sods.

In sheltered river valleys many more trees grew than on the open plains. Ranches located in the valleys usually had better buildings. The buildings had wooden walls and roofs, some even had wooden floors. Wooden buildings were bothered with fewer pests, such as rats and fleas. They were also easier to maintain. The best ranches were those with wooden buildings.

When cowboys returned to their ranches after the spring roundup, there were many different jobs for them to do during the summer. The job they liked least was called riding line. Each ranch had an area of land on which its cattle grazed. The ranch did not own this land, and several ranches might overlap. The ranches tried to keep their cattle on this area of land because it would make them easier to control. The cowboy riding line had to spend days on end riding along the imaginary line which marked the edge of the ranch's grazing land. He was expected to look for any strays that had wandered over the line. These he would drive back.

The line rider also had to keep an eye open for any tracks crossing into the ranch's area. These might mean trouble. In the early days of

cattle ranching, Indian raids were a very real threat. More than one cowboy was killed and his cattle stolen by Indians. Larger war parties might attack ranches, killing everybody they could find. Skirmishes between cowboys and Indians were fairly common. It was to deal with the Indians that the Texas Rangers were originally formed. In later years, with Indians confined to reservations, these raids ceased.

Most cowboys spent the summer riding around the range checking up on the cattle. If a cow or a steer was in trouble, the cowboy had to help it. One of the most difficult of these jobs was digging cattle out of bogs. Longhorns often stood in mud to find relief from the insects that buzzed around the plains. Sometimes a cow would become stuck in the mud. Cowboys had to haul her out with ropes. Once she was free, she was often so angry that she would then attack the cowboys who had just rescued her.

The insects also caused other problems. If a steer were injured somehow, a blowfly might lay its eggs in the wound. When the eggs hatched the worms fed on the steer, causing illness and even death. Whenever a cowboy saw an injured cow or steer, he had to rub ointment, often including carbolic acid, into the wound to kill the parasites.

Numerous other jobs also required attention during the summer. Cattle had to be kept away from locoweed and thick brush. Sick cattle had to be treated or isolated from the herd. The longhorns needed constant attention if they were to remain healthy.

Summer was also the time to catch, break, and train horses. Ranch hands would set off in large groups to catch wild mustangs. This was usually done by chasing the herd of wild horses into a prepared corral. Here they could be roped with ease. The initial breaking was often done by a cowboy particularly skilled at breaking horses. As soon as a horse would accept a saddle and rider, it was handed over to other cowboys to be trained.

The horses of a ranch were kept together in a

In the early days of the Far West, Texas was a lawless land and herds of cattle were often stolen by ruthless rustlers and Indian raiders. To combat this menace, the Texas Rangers were formed. They were tough men, able to ride all day from dawn to dusk during their hunt for wrongdoers. They wore no uniform but all knew how to handle a gun when the occasion arose.

group known as the remuda. Remuda de caballos is Spanish for "relay of horses." This remuda was looked after by a man called a wrangler.

Although the horses belonged to the ranch, each cowboy had his own string. This string numbered about six horses. It included horses skilled at cutting or roping and horses useful for their speed or endurance. Each day, the cowboys chose the horses from their string that they would need for the day's work.

Winter was the slow season for the cattle ranch. As bad weather approached, there was less and less work to do. Many cowboys were dismissed from the ranch during the winter because there was not enough work for them.

Those that remained worked at a variety of tasks. They spent many days inspecting and repairing their equipment. They wanted to make sure it would be ready for the next summer. Ranch buildings usually need repairs, and the cowboys also did this during the winter.

Occasionally, ranch hands needed to ride out to find the cattle. A herd might be stranded amid deep snow, while only a few miles away good grazing existed. The cowboys would drive the cattle to the fresh pasture. At other times, the cowboys would have to break the ice on ponds and streams so that the cattle could drink.

The cowboys who left the ranch spent winter in a variety of ways. During fair weather, they might hunt wolves. A bounty was paid on every wolf killed. A good hunter could earn a lot of money killing wolves. Other cowboys might drift into town looking for work.

Many cowboys, however, spent their time riding from ranch to ranch. Everybody knew they were out of work. The natural hospitality of the West was seen at its best in the winter. Any cowboy who turned up on a ranch was welcomed. The rancher and his hands were eager for news from neighboring ranches and the outside world. There might even be a few odd jobs for the drifter to do. The cowboy would stay for several days, with his food and lodging provided free. Then he would move on to the next ranch for a few days.

By the end of the winter, a drifter could find himself hundreds of miles from where he had started. As spring began to melt the snow, he would look for work on a new ranch. Most cowboys only worked at a ranch for a single season. By the next summer, they had moved on to another ranch.

THE LONG DRIVE

Driving the cattle to market was the most important job on any ranch. Without the money paid for the cattle, the ranch would fail and the cowboys lose their jobs. The trail drives were critical.

Once Joseph McCoy had established the practice of loading cattle onto railroad cars for the journey east, cattle drives became common. Ranchers all over the western plains drove their cattle to meet the railroad. Wherever cattle grazed, they were rounded up and driven to the railhead towns to be sold. The most important and impressive of these drives began in Texas.

After the spring roundups were completed, the prime four-year-old cattle were herded together for the drive. Sometimes a rancher would drive his cattle north himself. Other ranchers would employ a professional cattle trailer, or drover, to take over the herd.

The make-up of the herd was important. Fully grown cattle were the most profitable to drive, but they were the most difficult to keep together in an orderly mass. If a number of cows and their calves were included in the herd, the steers became easier to drive. Most herds were mixed in some way.

The size of the herds varied enormously. Small ranchers driving their own stock northward might only have about 500 head of cattle. The foremen of large ranches could have as many as 2,500 head. The drovers, who might be moving the longhorns of several ranches at once, could have even more. The average herd was between 2,000 and 3,000 head.

The herds set off after the spring roundup. At this time of year the fresh green grass was beginning to grow on the plains. The cattle had to be fed while they trekked north. Several hours each day would be spent grazing.

The need for as short a journey as possible

and the presence of good grass along the route meant that a number of trails were blazed. The most famous of these cattle trails was the Chisholm Trail. This route ran from the Red River Station, near the northern border of Texas, to the railroad at Abilene, Kansas.

Cattle came from all over Texas. Many herds had already covered hundreds of miles before they joined the Chisholm Trail for the 600-mile plod to Abilene. The trail was named after Jesse Chisholm, an early trader on the plains. He was the son of a Scottish father and a Cherokee Indian mother. He traced out the route from the Red River to Kansas just after the Civil War. Not too much later, hundreds of cowboys were trailing thousands of cattle along the route.

No matter where the herd started, the daily routines of the cowboys were very similar. Working as a cowboy on the trail was tough work. The typical outfit on the trail consisted of about a dozen men. The trail boss was in charge of the whole operation and was the

highest-paid man on the team. There would also be a wrangler responsible for driving the remuda of horses. Each herd was driven by about ten cowboys. Some were young and inexperienced. Others were old hands who had trailed before. The cowboys were paid according to their experience. About $40 a month was the average wage for a trail hand.

Finally there was the cook. The cook was in charge of more than cooking. He drove the chuck wagon and was responsible for pitching and striking camp each night. He also had to check that the stores were in good condition and ration them. The chuck wagon was vital to the success of any herd. It contained all the equipment needed for pitching camp at the end of the day. It also contained food for the hands to eat during the long weeks on the trail. This was usually coffee, flour, beans, sugar, and bacon. When they needed beef on the trail they killed a cow.

With these simple ingredients and a few others, the cook produced what became staple

The average herd of cattle driven north amounted to between 2,000 and 3,000 head.

Western food. One typical example of this style of cooking was sourdough bread. Each chuck wagon carried a sourdough barrel. In this the cook put a mixture of flour, water, and sugar. This was then allowed to ferment naturally. After a few days some of this mixture was scooped out and mixed with more flour and water to form a dough. This was left to rise before being baked. The result was sourdough bread. Each day, more flour and water were added to replace the mixture that had been used. This way the fermentation could continue to provide a starting scoop for the next day's dough.

Because beef slaughtered on the trail was likely to be fairly tough, it was usually stewed. These stews were made with any ingredients that were at hand and were cooked for quite a long time. They were always tasty. Of course, huge steaks were favorite items, when they were available. Only a small part of a tough longhorn was tender enough to grill as a steak,

so such feasts were rare. If the cowboys were able to shoot any game along the trail, it found its way to the chuck wagon.

The cook was the man to begin the day on the trail. At dawn, he roused the men from their sleep with the cry of "grub pi-i-ile," and gathered them together for breakfast. After a quick meal of sourdough and coffee, the cowboys packed up their bed rolls and stored them on the chuck wagon. They saddled their horses and set out for the herd. The cook meanwhile tidied up the camp, and stowed everything on the wagon. Then he could move out after the herd.

The cowboys, meanwhile, would already have begun driving the cattle forward. Each day the cattle were expected to cover about twelve miles. This allowed plenty of time for grazing and watering. Whenever the herd reached a stretch of particularly fine grass, they would be allowed to stop and graze. Often the grazing would go on for some hours. All the

Trail bosses were often at a loss to understand the Indians' sign language.

time the cowboys would ride around the herd to make sure that no animal strayed too far from the trail. With the grazing complete, the cowboys would gather the herd together again. Then the long, slow march would continue.

The long trails from Texas passed through Indian Territory. This land belonged to the Indian tribes. Strictly speaking, the Texans should not have been there at all. But the cowboys had to get their cattle to the railroad. The Indians decided to take advantage of the situation.

They began charging the Texans a fee for the right to drive their cattle across Indian country. This usually amounted to a few cents for each longhorn. Sometimes, the Indians took their payment in the form of cattle. The cowboys had to cut out several head from the herd and hand them over to the Indians. Negotiating with the Indians presented a problem. Few cowboys spoke Indian languages.

One cowboy recounted how he once tried to talk to an Indian chief in sign language. This failed and so he tried Spanish. The Indian at once called forward two braves who spoke Spanish. They demanded ten cattle. The trail boss told the cowboy to offer two. The talking went on for many hours. The Indians seemed unconcerned about the time. Eventually the

two parties agreed on a fee of four cattle. These cattle were paid to a small tribe. Larger and more powerful tribes demanded more.

Even after this toll had been paid, the Indians might return for more cattle. Sometimes young Indian braves would attack a herd and try to steal a few head for themselves. These swift raids, accompanied by war whoops and thundering hooves, were a serious problem to early drovers. From the 1870s on, the Indian attacks began to decrease. The cowboys, though, were always on the alert for them.

The large herds of cattle were worth a great deal of money, and drovers had to watch out for cattle rustlers. Large bands of rustlers would approach the herd and threaten to gun down the cowboys unless they handed over their cattle.

A favorite trick used by some rustlers was to pose as local ranchers who thought their cattle had joined the trail herd by accident. It was the custom to allow local ranchers to look for

their cattle. If they found a steer with their brand, they were allowed to take it. The rustlers, however, moved through the herd looking for any longhorn with a blurred or faint brand. They would claim such cattle as their own and drive them off.

It took a good trail boss to tell an honest rancher looking for lost cattle from a rustler. Even then, it might take some fast gunplay to drive the rustler away. The Texas Rangers were often found riding north of Texas in an effort to protect Texas cattle from rustlers.

Another obstacle that had to be overcome was the river crossing. Every herd had to cross several rivers on its way to market. There were no bridges on the plains in the cattle-driving days. Persuading longhorns to enter a river required a determined effort by the cowboys. If the sun was sparkling brightly on the water, the cattle would not take the plunge. If the river were flowing too quickly, the cattle would not enter. Sometimes, the longhorns would refuse to swim the river for what seemed no reason at all.

It could take hours of patient work to get the first cattle into the water. Once this was done, however, the rest of the herd would usually follow placidly. The cattle had to be kept moving during a river crossing. If the line of the herd became broken, the cowboys would have all the trouble of starting the cattle into the water again. Sometimes the cattle would panic in midstream and begin swimming around in circles. The cowboys then rode in among the cattle to direct and lead them to the far bank.

Other cattle might become stuck in mud or quicksand. The cowboys would have to rope these cattle and pull them out by brute force. One cowboy recorded that it took three whole days to get his herd across just one river.

When driving across open country, the herd took on a definite shape. Every cowboy had his job to do, and he knew it well.

At the front of the herd were the point riders.

The cowboys' gentle singing at night seemed to have a calming effect on the cattle.

These cowboys kept the lead cattle pointed in the right direction. Once this was done, the rest of the herd would follow in their steps. A little distance behind the point riders were the swing men. They helped turn the cattle, if the point men decided this had to be done. Otherwise the swing men joined the flankers in riding up and down the length of the herd. Their job was to keep the herd together in a narrow ribbon which could be controlled easily.

At the rear of the herd rode the drag men. The job of the drag men was to keep the stragglers from falling behind the herd. Riding drag was the most unpopular job on the trail. During hot days, the cattle kicked up so much dust that the drag riders almost choked and could barely see what they were doing. On wet days the hooves of the cattle kneaded the ground into a muddy mess. The drag men found themselves riding through a quagmire of mud. When the day's drive was over, the cowboys had to settle the cattle down for the night. The chuck wagon had been sent on ahead to the camping ground, and the cook was already

preparing the evening meal. On a stretch of flat ground, the cowboys halted the cattle. Slowly, so as not to frighten them, they drove the cattle together. When the cattle were in a tightly bunched group, they were allowed to lie down. After being driven a dozen miles, the cattle were usually only too content to rest.

Even at night the cowboys had to attend the cattle. In fact night was often the most dangerous time of all. Taking turns riding the night watch, the cowboys grabbed what sleep they could. As one old-time cowboy remarked, "If you expect to follow the trail, you must learn to do your sleeping in the winter."

The cowboys on watch rode slowly around and through the herd. They always sang to the cattle. The sound of a human voice rising and falling in song seemed to soothe the cattle and allow them to rest. Longhorns were easily frightened. A strange figure suddenly appearing from the dark might startle them. If the longhorn heard the steady approach of a human voice it would not be frightened. The continuous singing of the cowboys was also a sign

to the cattle that all was well. The great fear of any cowboy was a stampede of frightened cattle at night. If cattle were nervous, a stampede could be started by the slightest noise. Humid, warm nights kept the cattle awake. If a thunderstorm then broke, the longhorns would get to their feet and start to mill around. The rest of the cowboys would be called out of camp. Some would ride through the herd singing their hearts out. Other cowboys would try to separate the cattle to stop them milling. Often the cattle would calm down.

Sometimes something would shock the cattle. Perhaps it would be a clap of thunder or a flash of lightning. It could be a carelessly dropped pan. Even the moon suddenly shining across the plains could start a stampede. In a split second the cattle would be charging off at a frightening speed. The herd would become a heaving, running mass.

One cowboy described the noise of a stampede as follows: "The sound of the rushing hoofs is imposing enough at any time, but heard mingled and confused in the running in the dark it is something terrible. A loud cracking of hoofs comes through the fog of sound, and the mad rattling of the great horns in the crush as the cattle struggle to head out of the suffocating press behind them and on all sides."

If the cattle were allowed to run unchecked, disaster would follow. Cattle would trip and be trampled to death by those following. Others would tumble down sheer drops to their deaths. The whole herd could be scattered across a hundred square miles of prairie. The cattle that survived and were found might be injured and exhausted by the run. It would take days to get the herd together again.

As soon as a stampede started, the cowboys were in their saddles and away. It was dangerous work. If a cowboy's horse stumbled and fell, the man would be pounded to death in an instant. A cowboy could race his horse over a

Cowboys who fell during a stampede were often trampled to death by the terrified steers.

bluff in the dark and die in a fall. Stampedes were the most feared of all events on the cattle drives.

The only way cowboys could stop the terrible rush was to leap on their horses and catch the leading cattle. If these leaders could be reached, the cowboys could turn them. By swinging the lead cattle around in a huge circle, the cowboys could make them join up with the rear of the herd. The cattle would then be stampeding in a large ring. Gradually they would calm down, and the stampede would stop.

Eventually, after weeks or even months on the trail, the herd reached the railroad. In the early years most herds went to Abilene. Towns such as Dodge City, Wichita, and Ellsworth

later became the destinations of cattle drives. Here the cattle were sold and the cowboys given their wages.

Many tales are told of cowboys raising trouble as they celebrated their journey's end. In many cases this was true. After weeks of hard, punishing work the cowboys often rewarded themselves with drinking sprees. More often, though, a cowboy headed first for a barbershop. There the cowboy would have a shave and the first hot bath since the drive had started. Next in importance was a trip to a store. The clothes the cowboy had worn up the trail were by now ragged and torn. He needed a new set of clothes. Sometimes a new hat or pair of boots was bought as well. Only after all this had been done would the cowboy slip into a bar for a quiet drink and perhaps a game of cards.

Driving a herd of longhorns up the trail was long and tough work. The cowboy needed to relax when his work was all done.

THE END OF THE ERA

For the twenty years after the Civil War, the cowboy owned the West. There were a few miners and even some farmers to be seen, but the cowboy was the most important and by far the most impressive figure on the western plains.

Suddenly the age of the cowboy was over. Although they continued their work, cowboys no longer dominated the West. They found themselves sharing the land with their rivals the sheepherders.

The cattle ranchers had arrived on the range first, and they believed that cattle were the rightful grazers on the plains. Furthermore, the cattle ranchers pointed out, sheep destroyed pasture. They ate the grass roots as well as the leaves. Once sheep had grazed an area it could be useless for years. The extent to which sheep actually ruined pasture is not clear. But it is true that sheep crop grass so close to the ground that cattle cannot graze there until the grass has grown longer.

If a man tried to graze sheep on a section of range, it would not be long before a group of cowboys came visiting. In no uncertain terms the cowboys would tell the sheepherder to leave. If the man refused, his sheep could be shot. He might even be killed himself.

The struggle between sheep and cattle ranchers came to a head in Arizona in 1887. The Tewksbury family and the Grahams had been bickering for years. Then an astounded

A rancher would order a sheepman to remove his flock from the range. Refusal might result in the death of the sheep and the sheepman as well.

Graham cowboy saw the Tewksburys driving sheep into Pleasant Valley. For the next fifteen years the two families carried out an increasingly vicious vendetta. Men were gunned down mercilessly. Eventually, the entire Tewksbury and Graham families were wiped out.

In many ways these sheep wars were pointless. They were fought for control of range that was rapidly disappearing.

In 1874, Joseph Glidden, a farmer from Illinois, patented a new type of wire. It was strong, tough, and cheap. Armed with a ferocious array of spikes, it was called barbed wire.

The big ranchers were the first large-scale buyers of barbed wire. They realized that they could use it to stop cattle straying too far from the ranch. Their cattle would no longer become mixed with those of other ranches. Perhaps most important of all, by using barbed wire, the ranchers could keep various breeds of cattle separate. They could then breed their cattle more carefully. The tough longhorn no

longer had the range to himself. Newer and better breeds, such as the Hereford and the shorthorn, were brought in.

Barbed wire also brought trouble. Some ranchers fenced in land to which they had no right. They cut off other ranchers from land where their cattle had always grazed. Inevitably fences were cut. Fights broke out between fencers and cutters. Guns were drawn and men were killed either cutting or erecting fences.

Another use of barbed wire proved even worse for the cattle rancher. The small farmer began to use barbed wire to surround his land. Unlike ranchers fencing land which was not theirs, the farmers had law on their side.

According to the Homestead Act of 1862, any man who farmed 160 acres of unclaimed land could claim it for his own. By law, ranchers had no right to the land on which their cattle grazed. Any farmer could come and take it, and thousands of farmers did just that. Slowly but surely, much of the open range was disappearing beneath the plow.

That was the situation in the fall of 1886. That year the snows came early. Within a short time, the land was covered by snow so deep that the cattle could not find food. The ranchers had to use their precious stores of hay to keep their cattle alive. In January, warmer weather came to the plains. The emaciated cattle found some food.

Then a savage blizzard struck. For three days the blizzard raged. The driving snow buried cattle and covered the whole plains in a deep white blanket. No cowboy could leave his home without risking death. People could hear the painful cries of dying cattle. There was nothing anybody could do until the weather changed.

At long last, spring came to cattle country. Cowboys rode out to inspect the damage. They found many thousands of dead cattle. More than half the cattle were dead.

HOME ON THE RANGE

There are still cattle ranches in the West and cowboys to work on them. Many changes have come to the cowboy's way of life over the years, but many things remain the same. Although he may use a truck to ride the line, he still has to know how to ride and rope.

The cattle he ropes are very different from those caught in the Texas cow hunts of the 1860s. Few longhorns are left, and it is probably just as well. Longhorns were large, tough, and aggressive. They had to survive on the plains during the long years when they ran wild. Their aggressive streak and huge horns helped them fend off attacks from wolves and pumas. They had the strength to wander over the range, seeking better pastures and fresh water.

The cattle that have replaced the longhorns have none of these qualities. They do not need them. They no longer roam the open range. Instead they graze on broad pastures of grassland, fenced in and tightly controlled. The cowboys can carefully nurse their pasture. The cattle are only allowed to graze on the grass when it is in the peak of condition.

During the winter, hay and feed is distributed to the cattle. They do not need to travel long distances to search for their food. It is handed to them. In really severe weather, cattle may even be brought into shelter.

Today's cattle do not need to be as tough as the longhorns. This has enabled ranchers to start raising cattle that are easier to handle and give better meat. Herefords, Durhams, and Angus cattle all found their way onto the plains to replace the longhorns. Some large ranches even started breeding their own cattle. The King Ranch in Texas has raised a sturdy breed of cattle named Santa Gertrudis. These are a cross between Brahmas and shorthorns.

Also very different is the life of the average cowboy. He now lives in comfortable rooms. The flea-infested, damp dugouts are no more. With modern roads and automobiles, ranches are no longer isolated. Cowboys can watch television when off duty. They can climb into a truck and travel to town for the evening. A century ago such a journey might have taken several days.

There is a tendency for people who have never roped a calf to dress like a cowboy. Many people on

Cattle are still branded on the hip by today's cowboys. (*Panhandle Plains Historical Museum*).

the western plains sport Stetsons, high boots, and bandannas. But if you put these people alongside the real range riders, you can easily tell the difference. A real cowboy wears his clothes with an easy grace, as if they were made for him. In a way, they were.

On the other hand, many parts of a cowboy's life have stayed the same. He still performs hard physical work. He rises early in the morning to begin the day's work. Though he might get into a truck, or even a helicopter, the cowboy still has his horse. For working cattle on the grasslands there is still nothing better than a good cow horse.

When a cowboy has to drive cattle out of the bush or separate one steer from the herd, he does it in the same old fashioned way. On horseback, the cowboy will carefully position himself between the cow and the herd. When the cow is far enough away from the other cattle, the cowboy throws his lariat to drop over the cow's head. In many ways roping is easier today. Modern breeds of cattle have shorter horns than the old Texas longhorns. Getting a rope to fall over the horns is far less difficult than it used to be.

As in the great days of the cowboys, roping is most often done during the spring roundup. In the old days the main reason for a roundup was to separate the cattle belonging to each rancher from each other. Today, the open range does not exist and the cattle no longer become mixed together. Yet the spring roundup still is a strong feature of the cowboy's year.

When the cattle are gathered together, the work begins. The new calves are cut out. They are branded on the hip with the brand of the ranch. This is no longer done to stop them being mixed up with another herd. It is the traditional stamp of ownership.

These branding irons have changed remarkably little since the great days of the cowboy. The handle is a long iron rod, and at its end is the brand. This consists of a pattern of iron which will leave the mark of the brand pattern. The irons are heated in a fire until they are glowing red hot. The branding iron is then pressed firmly onto the hip of the young calf. The hair is burned away and the skin singed.

No hair ever grows on the singed skin. The brand mark remains on the steer for the rest of its life. If the animal is sold, the rancher erases the brand with a recognized counter brand. The buyer then adds his own brand. Some cattle may end their days with half a dozen different brands on their hides.

The traveler out West may still see cowboys chasing cattle across the prairie. Cowboys still live on ranches. But there are very few cowboys today compared to the numbers found a hundred years ago. The plains no longer belong exclusively to the cowboys. They have lost much of this land to sheep ranchers, farmers, and housing developments. The great herds and the long trails may be gone forever, but the cowboy lives on.

RAILROADERS

G. CAMPION

RAILROADERS

Although it may seem surprising to us now, railways were in use four hundred years ago in the European country of Transylvania.

They were wooden tramways. Two hundred years later, similar wooden railways were still being used in England to transport coal from the mines to loading depots along riversides. The coal trucks were pulled by men or horses, because no form of steam, gas, or electrical power was available

By 1804, the wooden rails had been replaced by metal ones, but the trucks were still being hauled by men and horses. Then an Englishman named Richard Trevithick proudly exhibited his invention, a double-acting high-pressure steam engine and a steam road locomotive.

Unfortunately, because cast-iron is a brittle metal, the first locomotives were so heavy that they broke down often and Trevithick was laughed at and mocked by many people.

Then along came two Englishmen, George Stephenson and his son, Robert. They were determined to overcome all resistance to the use of steam locomotives as a new form of transport.

They constructed the first locomotive with a multi-tubular boiler and named it *Rocket*. In 1829, at Rainhill in England, the *Rocket* reached a maximum speed of 29 miles per hour. Railroads as we know them today had come to stay. Today's locomotives travel much faster, usually around 100 miles per hour.

THE IRON HORSE

At the time George and Robert Stephenson invented their *Rocket*, people in the eastern part of America were planning railroads. But at that time their plans did not include the use of steam power. They expected the cars to be pulled by horses along wooden tracks.

When it became known that steam-powered locomotives had been invented in England, a Horatio Allen, a young engineer who worked for the Delaware and Hudson Canal Company, went to England to see these wonder engines. They were called Iron Horses. He was so impressed that he ordered four of them. On May 13, 1829, the first English locomotive arrived in New York City.

Some people thought it looked like a huge grasshopper. On the front was the face of a big, fierce-looking lion. The engine's name was *The Stourbridge Lion* because it had been built by a company in Stourbridge, England.

Horatio Allen brought his *Lion* to life with steam, and thousands of people flocked to see the curious locomotive. But there were no tracks on which to run it, so Allen shipped it by river and canal to Honesdale, Pennsylvania. There he gave it a trial run on a flimsy wooden track. The run was successful, and Horatio Allen became the first man to make a trip on a steam engine operated on the tracks of an American railroad.

The Iron Horse had come to stay. From then on the design of steam engines rapidly improved and steel rails replaced wooden tracks.

Horatio Allen later became the chief engineer of the South Carolina Railroad Company. He designed a new American locomotive in Charleston, South Carolina. Named *Best Friend of Charleston*, it had a vertical boiler shaped like a wine bottle. It was America's first regular passenger train and it operated over what was then the longest railroad in the world — 136 miles.

Unfortunately, the fireman operating it one June day in 1831 knew nothing about the power of steam. He became annoyed by the hissing of the safety valve, and he tied down the lever. The pressure of steam built up, and the *Best Friend of Charleston* exploded, killing

The Stourbridge Lion was the first locomotive to be seen in New York. The year was 1829.

the fireman and badly scalding the engineer.

Allen also designed the first "headlight." It was a flat car placed in front of the engine, containing a wood fire burning in sand.

The early American trains were called puffers because of the sound they made. Traveling by rail in those days was not only uncomfortable but dangerous for people riding in open flat cars. Blazing sparks from the smoke stacks showered down on them and set fire to their clothing. Some people put up umbrellas to fend off the flying embers but soon found out this was not a good idea, since the umbrellas caught fire. They were enveloped in clouds of black smoke. When the engine lurched forward or braked with a jerk, passengers were flung out of their seats, which in those days were wooden benches. They landed either on the floor or on top of each other. The trains also tended to jump the track when rounding a curve.

In spite of all the discomfort and danger, traveling by train was something new and exciting. People eagerly crowded into the carriages and onto the open cars to experience the thrill of riding on a train pulled by an Iron Horse.

A Pony Express rider races toward a relay station.

EARLY TRANSPORT

The railroads finally won the West, but other forms of transportation also have their pride of place in American history. In April 1860, the famous Pony Express was the means of transporting mail quickly from St. Joseph, Missouri, to San Francisco, a distance of some 2,000 miles. It took 10 days. Mail was carried by 120 courageous young riders who faced danger from war parties, bandits, blizzards, and raging rivers.

Rider galloped up to relay stations along the route, threw their mail pouches onto a waiting horse, and raced off again, all within two minutes. After riding a certain distance a rider handed his mail over to the next rider waiting at another station.

The Pony Express only lasted a year, because a transcontinental telegraph put them out of service. The founders, Russell, Majors, and Waddell, were heavily in debt. The fees charged for carrying 35,000 items of mail did not cover the cost of running the service.

American industry was growing fast, and the field of transportation was in the lead. A railroad was soon to follow the route of the Pony riders across the Plains and mountains.

The era of the river steamboat started in 1811 and lasted for 60 years. Steamboats were fast, flat-bottomed boats with three or four tiers of decks. They offered passengers every luxury available at the time. Proudly they chugged up and down the Mississippi, Missouri, and other western rivers, smoke billowing from their long funnels. By 1846 there were almost 2,000 steamboats on western rivers, and they were carrying $400 million worth of freight.

Twenty years before a railroad ever spanned the continent, freight wagons pulled by teams of oxen transported goods from Missouri to California in four months. Stagecoaches also carried passengers and mail across the West.

John Butterfield started the famous Overland Mail. His Concord stagecoaches took 24 days to complete the journey from St. Louis. They traveled through desert and mountainous country, and through the home of half a million Indians who were not always friendly.

Russell, Majors, and Waddell also ran a stage line and freight wagons, but the greatest of all freight companies was The American Express Company. It shipped all kinds of goods worth millions of dollars across the West. It invented the C.O.D. (cash on delivery) system, which is still used today. From stagecoaches, the company moved into railroads and then banking. The famous Wells Fargo joined forces with The American Express Company in 1852, and today it is still a part of American Express. Instead of Concord coaches pulled by a team of six horses, though, Wells Fargo uses heavily armored trucks painted the traditional Wells Fargo red.

Pony Express riders, steamboats, freight wagons, and stagecoaches all pointed the way for the great railroads across the West.

THE WAY TO THE WEST

December 9, 1852, was the first time that anyone had ridden on a train west of the Mississippi River. Although the locomotive was owned by the Pacific Railroad of Missouri and was named *The Pacific*, it did not go anywhere near the West Coast. The entire distance it chugged its way along was a five-mile stretch of track running westward from St. Louis, Missouri. But it was the start of the rails going westward.

For many years people had been talking about a transcontinental railroad. At the time it seemed like an impossible dream, just as putting men on the moon once seemed impossible. The railroad dream became a reality in 1869, and 100 years later, in 1969, man set foot on the moon.

Building a railroad spanning 2,000 miles from Missouri to California was the greatest engineering feat in American history.

The first big problem was to find a suitable route across America. It would have to cross the vast plains, inhabited by thousands of Indians and millions of buffalo. It would have to climb up and over high mountain ranges and cross burning deserts.

The Civil War had started in 1861, and the North and South were split over the slavery issue and states' rights. Each side had its own idea as to where a railroad should be built.

Army engineers and politicians suggested different routes, some favoring the trails blazed by the early explorers, fur trappers, and Indian traders. The Indian trails across the West discovered by frontiersmen were not always suitable for the laying of railroad tracks.

Two brilliant surveyors, Theodore Judah and Major General Grenville Dodge, finally mapped out an acceptable route for the transcontinental railroad. The route they chose followed the basic path of the Emigrant Trail, along which pioneers and miners had traveled to reach California. It was not an easy route, as it meant going over the Sierra Nevada and Rocky Mountains, blasting through rock and granite to make tunnels and tracks on which to lay the rails.

The path they chose for the railroad would join the Pacific coast to more than 30,000 miles of track existing at that time in the Eastern states.

Theodore Judah surveyed the route east from Sacramento, California. Grenville Dodge surveyed it from Omaha, Nebraska, westward. The Pacific Railroad Act was drawn up largely through Judah's efforts, and President Lincoln signed it in July of 1862. The transcontinental railroad would be built by two companies, the Central Pacific and Union Pacific.

The Central Pacific broke ground at Sacramento in January 1863 and the Union Pacific at Omaha in the December of that year.

General Grenville M. Dodge was the chief engineer for the Union Pacific, the railroad which was built from Omaha in the east to the Far West. Starting in 1865, it was completed in 1869 after four years of constant dangers and hardship.

But before the actual construction could start, a lot of money was needed and land had to be obtained. By July 1865, however, when the Civil War had ended, there was sufficient money and land for the mammoth project to go ahead.

Much of the land over which the railroad would run was stolen from the Indians. It was the grazing ground of their buffalo. Whenever they got the chance, the enraged warriors would gallop alongside a train and shoot at the hated Iron Horse.

The construction gangs of the Union Pacific were made up of a mixed bunch of tough men. There were many Irish and some British and Germans. There were Civil War veterans from both the North and South and freed slaves.

Workers had to be tough to lay miles of track. The railroad took four years to build, and there was fierce competition between the crews of both railroads as to who laid the most track at one time. In April 1869, just before the two railroads joined, both the Central and the Union Pacific claimed the laying of 10 miles of track in one day, a mighty feat indeed.

THE ATTACK AT PLUM CREEK

*I*t did not take the Indians long to realize that the Iron Horse was their greatest enemy.

Gangs of railroad workers poured into western Nebraska and southeastern Wyoming in the hundreds. They invaded the hunting grounds of the Sioux and Cheyennes as they laid the tracks of the Union Pacific. The furious Indians sounded their war drums, donned their war paint, and attacked the invaders.

They took their revenge out on the telegraph wires, tearing them down. They believed the humming of the wires was bad medicine and would harm them. They ripped up the iron rails. They attacked trains and killed passengers. They took whatever goods the train was carrying.

One famous incident took place at Plum Creek, Nebraska, on August 6, 1867.

A war party of Cheyennes led by their chief, Turkey Leg, was riding along an ancient Indian trail when they came across the tracks of the Union Pacific. Lying alongside the rails was a pile of ties, or sleepers. That was just what the warriors needed to cause a wreck.

Their hearts were filled with anger because they were escaping from an army patrol that was scouring the territory for warring Indians. Here was the chance they had been waiting for. They made a barricade of the ties and laid them across the track. Ripping the wires from a nearby telegraph pole, they lashed the ties to the rails.

They had no idea when a train would be coming along, but they were prepared to wait hours if necessary. So they took cover in some bushes close by and waited.

Some miles away at Plum Creek Station, the telegraph repairman, who was a young Englishman by the name of William Thompson, noticed that the line had gone dead. It was his job to see that the telegraph was working at all times on his section of the railroad. He sprang into action, for he had to find the break in the line and repair it as quickly as possible.

He and five section hands jumped on a hand-pump car loaded with a spool of new wire, repair tools and six Spencer rifles, and set off down the track.

It was dark by then and they were going at speed, so they never saw the barricade. The hand-pump car smashed into it, and all six men went flying through the air, landing heavily on the ground.

The next instant the Cheyennes, uttering harsh war cries, rushed from their hiding place with rifles blazing. The five section hands were killed outright. Thompson staggered to his feet, groping for one of the Spencers that had been flung out of the car. Before he could reach it he was shot in the arm by a Cheyenne and knocked to the ground.

Unfortunately for the young man, he had long blonde hair, and this was something no warrior could resist. The next minute Thompson's scalp was being lifted.

He lay still and pretended to be dead. Through pain-filled eyes he watched the war party picking up the tools and waited for a chance to crawl away.

With the tools and the spool of wire from the pump car, the Indians improved their ambush. They unbolted two rails, wrenched them up, and with much grunting and heaving managed to bend them in two. They lashed them up with wire and then laid them across the track.

While they were doing this, Thompson crawled silently away.

The night freight train was pounding up from the east and the waiting Cheyennes saw its faint oil-fired head lamp in the distance. They brandished their rifles over their heads.

Like Thompson, the engine driver failed to see the barricade until it was too late. The engine crashed into it, killing him and the fireman.

At the end of the train the construction crew leapt out of the carriage and hearing Indian war cries, they tore away in the darkness and made their escape back to Plum Creek. On the way they managed to flag down a following freight train just in time to avoid a second collision.

Meanwhile, at the wreck, the Indians set about looting the train and to their joy found a barrel of whiskey. They carried off their loot and disappeared into the night, triumphant at their victory over the hated enemy.

The hand-pump car smashed into the barricade as a yelling mob of Cheyennes sped forward. They intended to kill all the railroad men without mercy. Only one man was to survive.

Somehow William Thompson found the strength to crawl for miles before he was rescued and taken to a doctor. He survived his terrible ordeal and later returned to his job.

The Union Pacific construction crews faced danger from the hostile Indians, but their rivals, the Central Pacific, faced a different kind of danger. For them, danger came in the form of accidents and severe weather conditions when laying tracks over the formidable Sierra Mountains and across the parched deserts.

The Indians were fighting for their lives, their land, and their buffalo. They had seen their great herds slaughtered by thousands by buffalo hunters. Now the Iron Horse had

The tracklayers were drilled relentlessly until they could spike down track so speedily that finally they reached the amazing rate of ten miles per day. The workers were often bribed to work faster with extra tobacco and double wages.

invaded their land, bringing another danger to their buffalo. A new sport had sprung up among the white men. As the great shaggy beasts quietly grazed alongside the railroad tracks, passengers shot them with rifles from the moving trains.

In frustration, the Indians kept up their attacks on the construction crews and the situation got so bad the U.S. Indian-Fighting Army was called in to protect the railroad workers. By 1868, nearly 5,000 soldiers were patrolling along and around the tracks. In despair, the Sioux and Cheyenne, two mighty Plains tribes, knew their days were numbered. Eventually they would all be rounded up and placed on reservations. Their freedom, their land, and their buffalo would be taken away from them forever.

To protect the construction crews as they worked on the railroads, the U.S. Indian-Fighting Army was sent in and one of the commanding officers was none other than that well-known cavalier of the Plains, Lt. Col. George A. Custer.

TRACKS ACROSS THE WEST

General Grenville Dodge, was chief engineer of the Union Pacific. John (Jack) Casement, another Civil War general, was the track-laying boss. Although Jack was only five feet, four inches tall, he was a tough commander and quickly earned the respect of the big, burly men in the track-laying gangs. His brother, Dan, assisted him and was even shorter. Like Jack, though, no one ever tangled with him.

Jack Casement signed a contract with Thomas C. Durant, who was vice-president and general manager of the Union Pacific, to lay track for $750 a mile. He drilled his men relentlessly until they could spike down track speedily and with precision. In fact, no one had ever used such an efficient rail-laying routine before.

Men worked ahead of the train, grading and leveling the road-bed and dropping the ties into place, five for each section of track.

Lightweight carts loaded with 16 rails, spikes, bolts, and rail couplings (called fish-plates), were each hauled by a galloping horse to the newest sections of track. Men working in pairs lifted each rail, which weighed between 500 to 700 pounds, out of the cart, ran forward, and as the foreman yelled "Down!" they dropped the rail onto the ties. Men with a notched wooden gauge spaced each pair of rails at four feet, eight and one half inches apart. Then clampers fixed the rails in place and the spike men swung their mauls (long-handled hammers) and knocked in the spikes.

At first the crews laid a mile of track a day, but when the rival crews of the Union Pacific and Central Pacific got closer to each other the pace quickened to two, three, and even more miles a day. Jack Casement was known to offer bribes to his men ranging from extra tobacco to double pay if they would work faster.

The work train was the nerve center of the track-laying operation. It moved along the freshly laid track carrying the necessary supplies for the laying of track ahead of it. It was pushed by an engine, instead of being pulled. In front were flat cars carrying all the tools and a blacksmith shop. Then came the bunkhouse-on-wheels, three huge boxcars, 85 feet long with three tiers of bunks where some 300 to 400 men slept. After that came the dining car, a car divided into a kitchen, washroom and storeroom, a car for the carpenter's shop, and a car for the engineer's office and the telegrapher and his equipment. It was like a miniature town on wheels.

The railroad worker's life was not an easy one. The pay was only a few dollars a day. The food was a steady diet of beef, beans, pie, bread, and coffee. The work was back-breaking and the men toiled in freezing cold and burning heat. There was always the threat of accidents and the fear of Indian attacks.

On one occasion Grenville Dodge was having a meeting with several government officials in his private car on a train at the end of a track. They were at a camp 100 miles west of Overton, Nebraska. A war party of Sioux suddenly swooped down on the camp. Workmen, used to such attacks, dropped their tools and grabbed their rifles, which were always close at hand, and blazed away at the warriors.

General Dodge ran out of his car, firing his revolver and encouraging his men. The Indians soon retreated to a nearby ravine, and Dodge was all for going after them but the men refused. They told him they had to defend themselves against attack, but they were paid to build a railroad, not to fight Indians.

These mobile towns were made up of gamblers, saloonkeepers, thieves, and dance hall girls. They were all out to make a "fast buck" by taking from the rail workers their hard-earned wages.

The track layers had nothing to amuse or entertain them at the end of a tough day's work. When the camp followers came along, the men could not get to the tents fast enough on payday to drink and gamble their wages away. Some of the dance hall girls carried little derringer pistols and held up the workers before they even reached the tents.

Fights broke out among the railmen, gamblers, and saloonkeepers. Many of them were severely hurt, and some were even killed.

Grenville Dodge, who ran his construction crews like a military operation, did not interfere with his men losing their money. What

With little to amuse them at the end of a day's work, the reckless railroad crews drank and gambled away their hard-earned wages.

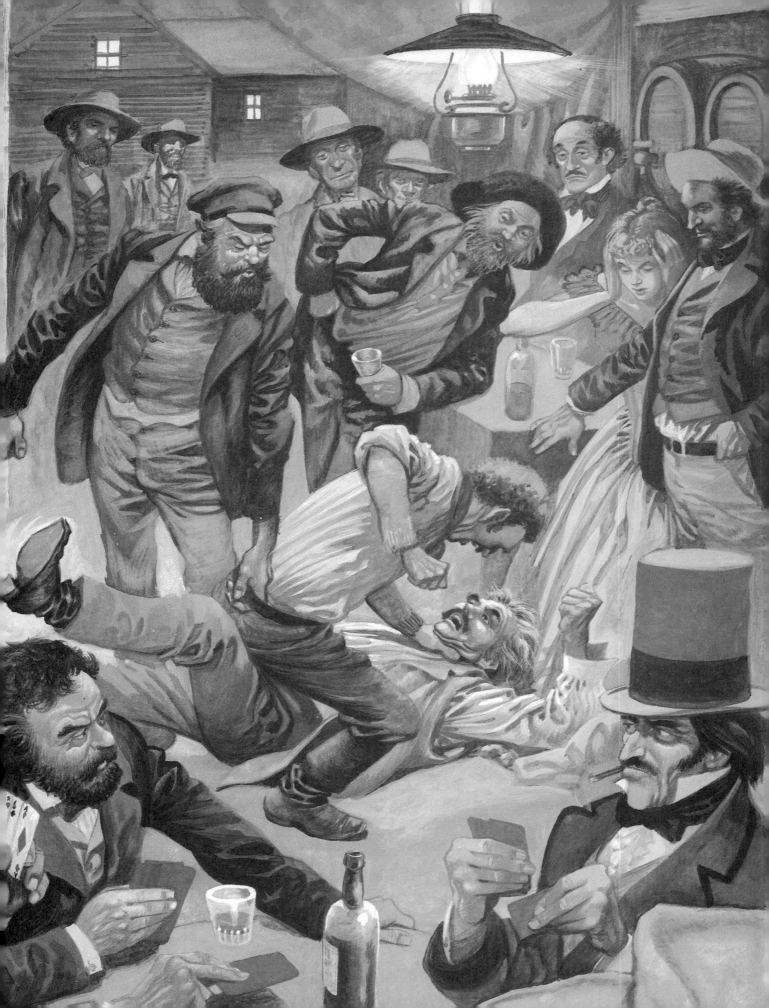

they did with their pay was their own business. But when it came to his men being wounded or killed, he put his foot down. It was difficult enough to get hard-working crews, and he was not going to lose men at the makeshift towns that sprang up around his Union Pacific. He asked Jack Casement to do something about it.

Casement chose a few of his rough, burly, muscled men, and they started visiting the gambling tents and saloons. After a few fights and shootings, the people who operated the lawless towns got the message. The railmen still visited the tents and lost their money gambling or spent it on alcohol, but apart from a few brawls, the killing and serious wounding stopped. Casement continued his clean-up routine wherever the tent towns sprang up.

The weather was another hazard the railmen had to face. Summer storms could become violent with torrential rains, roaring thunder, and vivid lightning. Then came the snow of winter. The winter of 1867–68 was the worst on record. Winds called "blue northers" blew in from Canada, bringing tons of snow and halting the work of the Union Pacific altogether.

In January the Missouri River was frozen 16 inches thick at Omaha, strong enough to take the weight of an engine. Jack Casement decided to make good use of the frozen river.

Large supplies of materials he needed were stored on the opposite bank of the Missouri. Rather than waste time waiting for the ice to thaw so the materials could be ferried across the river, he laid temporary rails on the ice and was able to bring the supplies across easily and quickly.

After that came the spring thaw, which sent the melting snow rushing down the mountains and flooding the plains. The damage was heartbreaking to the railroad workers who saw miles of track, bridges, telegraph lines, and embankments all washed away. Work had to begin all over again.

Thomas C. Durant was in charge of the financing of the Union Pacific and was known to keep a good share of the money for himself. He wanted to extend the route mapped out by General Dodge in order to get more money from the government. When Dodge heard about it, he was able to prevent Durant's proposed scheme. Construction went ahead as planned.

The transportation of building materials for the railroad to the railhead was made much easier when the Chicago and Northwestern Railroad brought its tracks to the Missouri

River. Materials were ferried across the river to Omaha and were then loaded onto cars and taken down the track to where they were needed.

Getting sufficient wood for the ties was also made easier as the Union Pacific moved westward. Before reaching Wyoming, Jack Casement sent 1800 woodchoppers and haulers to the forests of Wyoming. By the time the rails reached the boundary of that vast territory, 100,000 ties were ready and waiting.

As the laying of track extended westward from Omaha, so people intent on making money began flocking to where construction crews had their camps. Tent towns sprang up and moved across the West, following the railroad workers.

Some of the mobile camp towns remained where they were as settlers in the thousands arrived on trains from the East and needed somewhere to live. Towns such as North Platte, Julesburg, Cheyenne, and Laramie became permanent settlements.

By present-day standards, these frontier towns were rough and wild at first. Soon, though, lawmen moved in and kept peace with their six-guns.

Herds of buffalo would often charge across the tracks, bringing the trains to a jolting halt.

THE STAMPEDE

Stampeding buffalo followed a leader. Wherever it ran, they were close behind, shaking the ground with the pounding of their hooves. If a train frightened them, they would often race alongside it, overtake it, and run across the track right in its path, bringing the train to a halt. These instances gave any passengers with rifles the chance to get in some shooting. With so many animals at close range, they could kill a great number in a short time.

After several trains had been held up by buffalo crossing the tracks, a water-spouting device was fitted to the engine in an attempt to chase the animals off. The jet of water was strong enough to stop a beast in its tracks, which would cause confusion in the herd.

They often turned to milling around in circles on either side of the track, with the moving train between them.

On one occasion Thomas Durant took a party of celebrities by train to see construction crews at work on the line a couple of hundred miles west of Omaha. After watching the sweating workers laying the rails and banging in the spikes, they all retired to the train for a meal of roast duck and champagne. Afterwards, Durant staged a buffalo hunt for the benefit of his guests. It was probably a shoot from the train windows, because if there were any buffalo grazing nearby the guests could easily have scared them into stampeding alongside the train.

There was a manpower shortage in California so the Central Pacific Railroad hired Chinese workers. To everyone's astonishment, the Chinese proved to be brave and reliable. As time went on, thousands of these tough Orientals were hired.

THE CENTRAL PACIFIC

Charles Crocker was the general superintendent of the Central Pacific Railroad. He was a big, tough man, always out on site directing construction and frequently grabbing a shovel or a pick when an extra hand was needed. It was his job to build the railroad eastward from California across the Sierra Nevada Mountains to link up with the Union Pacific, which was heading across endless plains toward the Rocky Mountains.

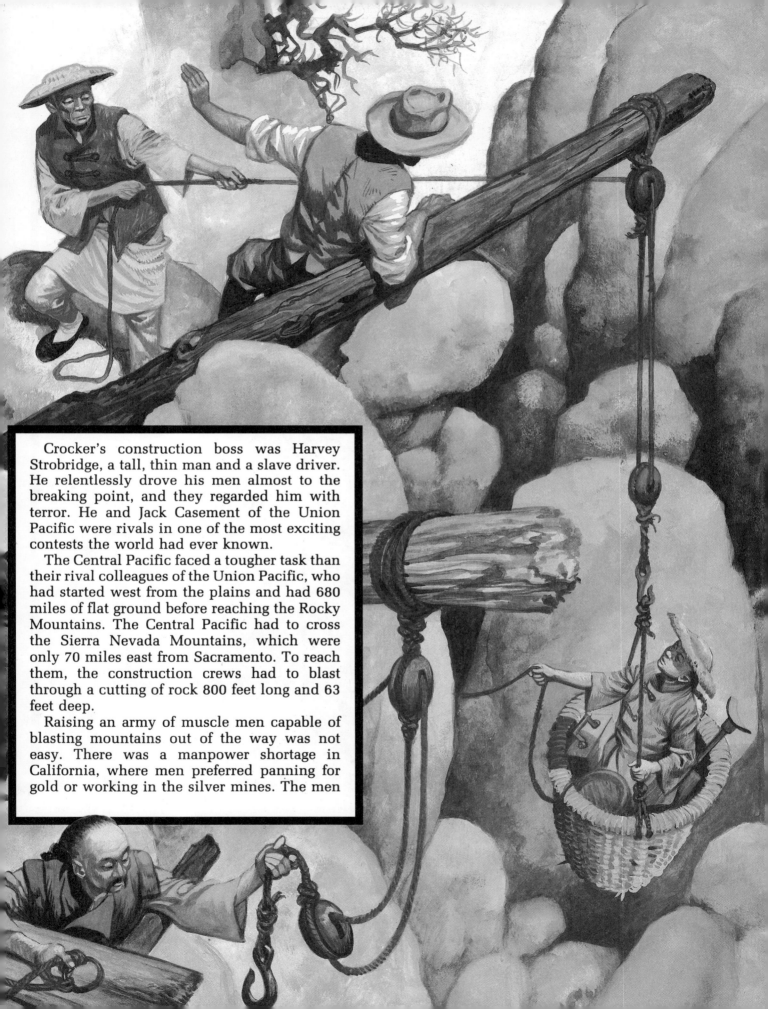

Crocker's construction boss was Harvey Strobridge, a tall, thin man and a slave driver. He relentlessly drove his men almost to the breaking point, and they regarded him with terror. He and Jack Casement of the Union Pacific were rivals in one of the most exciting contests the world had ever known.

The Central Pacific faced a tougher task than their rival colleagues of the Union Pacific, who had started west from the plains and had 680 miles of flat ground before reaching the Rocky Mountains. The Central Pacific had to cross the Sierra Nevada Mountains, which were only 70 miles east from Sacramento. To reach them, the construction crews had to blast through a cutting of rock 800 feet long and 63 feet deep.

Raising an army of muscle men capable of blasting mountains out of the way was not easy. There was a manpower shortage in California, where men preferred panning for gold or working in the silver mines. The men

Crocker did sign on were mostly Irish immigrants. And then he got an idea that saved the situation: he would hire Chinese workers.

Many Chinese had come to California in search of gold. When the gold rush years ended, hundreds of them stayed on, working as house servants and in restaurants, or as laborers. They were hated and persecuted by the white people because they worked for less money and worked harder. People made fun of their blue cotton trousers, their conical straw hats, and their pigtails.

When Crocker ordered Strobridge to hire 50 Chinese on a trial basis, the construction boss nearly exploded. He was not going to have little Orientals work for him. They ate bamboo shoots and rice and drank tea and looked so frail a puff of wind would blow them over. But Crocker was his boss, so he had to obey orders.

To everyone's astonishment the little Chinese, who averaged under five feet tall, proved brave, tough, reliable workers, willing to tackle any job no matter how hard. In time even Strobridge came to respect them, and Crocker hired thousands of Chinese, even bringing them directly from China.

Fifty-seven miles out from Sacramento the Chinese, who were known as "Crocker's Pets," proved they were as courageous as they were reliable. The surveyors had decided that the rails would have to go along a ledge cut around a huge rocky overlay jutting out from the side of a mountain, 1,400 feet above a river.

Strobridge knew his Chinese crew never refused to do a job, so he set them to do an extremely dangerous task. They wove baskets of reeds large enough to hold a man armed with an iron hand drill, a sledge, and a keg of black powder. The workers were lowered down the cliff face in the baskets. Swaying perilously against the side of the mountain, they drilled and pounded two-and-a-half-inch-wide holes in the rock. They filled the holes with powder and set fuses in them. They were then hauled up to safety just before the explosions rocked the gorge.

The Chinese loved firecrackers because they believed the noise frightened away devils, and they actually enjoyed the deafening ex-

During the snow-swept winter of 1876-1877, many Chinese tracklayers were killed by avalanches. Doggedly, the survivors worked on, determined that nothing would stand in their way. The Central Pacific _would_ go through.

plosions in spite of the dangers involved.

Slowly and steadily they blasted through the solid rock and made the required ledge without losing a single man.

After their bravery in blasting a ledge around the rocky outlay, "Crocker's Pets" earned the respect of all the white railroad men. They were amazed at the stamina of the frail-looking little Chinese and were amused that they bathed every day and drank quantities of hot tea. It was tea made with boiling water that helped to prevent the Chinese from getting sick. The white workers drank ditch water and frequently suffered from stomach upsets.

Crocker had faith in them right from the start. He had reasoned that if the Chinese could build the largest piece of masonry in the world, the Great Wall of China, then they could build a railroad. And he was right. Eight thousand workers were put to work on the Summit Tunnel high in the Sierra Nevada Mountains, and 6,000 of them were Chinese. Nine tunnels had to be hollowed out of granite and rock in order for the track to be laid up and through the mountains and down the long steep eastern slope of the mountain range.

The winter of 1866-67 was a terrible one in the Sierras. There were 44 blizzards, one lasting 13 days with no letup. Snow piled up 10 feet high and, blown by strong winds, formed an overhanging mass at the edge of the mountain. The weight of the hardened snow caused it to move, and a great avalanche swept men, equipment, and the workers' pitiful dwellings down into the canyon below. Many Chinese, powerless to save themselves, were killed as they went hurtling down the mountain, caught up in the violent force of the rushing snow.

The Chinese working in the tunnels tackled the granite by standing shoulder to shoulder and chipping away with their picks, a few inches a day. During that time nitroglycerin, a liquid explosive, was discovered. It was more powerful than black powder, and the task of blasting and moving tons of rock was sped up. But there were many accidents.

Strobridge lost his right eye by impatiently going to see why an explosion had not occurred. It went off, and he was caught in the blast. He had to wear a patch over his eye and the Chinese called him "One Eye Bossy Man."

Once a way was cleared through and over the Sierras, gangs of 500 workers followed, hauling huge log sleds that carried three locomotives,

40 cars, and enough rails to cover the mountain route.

Up ahead, the graders were hacking out cuttings and building high timber trestle embankments to prevent the trains from having to climb or descend too sharply. Gangs of Chinese hauled away rock and earth in wheelbarrows and dump carts.

By the spring of 1868 the Central Pacific was through the mountains and the crews had to face the heat of the Nevada desert. Laying track on the flat was far easier than up in the Sierras, though.

The lines of the Central Pacific and Union Pacific were getting closer, but in the early months of 1869 no meeting place had been decided. But the race was on in earnest.

The Union Pacific had to cross the Rocky Mountains, but only had to dig four tunnels. The Central Pacific had to dig 15 tunnels in all. The Echo Summit in the Wasatch Range in Utah was the most difficult to tackle. In their haste to beat their rivals, the Union Pacific construction crews built a temporary looping bypass around the summit instead of tunneling through it. They planned to build the tunnel later.

The converging construction gangs met in the American desert. They were only 50 miles apart, but still no effort was made by the leaders to choose a place for the link-up. The Central Pacific was headed in the direction of Ogden, but the Union Pacific did not seem to know where it was going. Their survey lines overlapped for some miles, and when the grading gangs met and went on to pass each other, they were so close they had to dodge the earth thrown up by the other's blasting charges.

When President Grant heard of this ridiculous situation, he summoned Grenville Dodge to Washington and told him to arrange a meeting with the representatives of both companies and decide where their tracks were to link up.

A meeting was held, and Promontory Point, Utah, was decided upon. It was 56 miles west of Ogden, a waterless basin of sagebrush with mountains on three sides. The date was set for May 8, 1869.

The tracks of the Central Pacific reached Promontory Point on April 30. Charles Crocker and his long-suffering Californians had won the race. They were waiting to jeer and boo the Union Pacific crews when they came into view a week later.

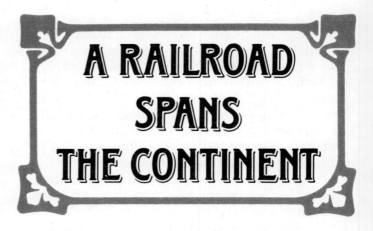

A RAILROAD SPANS THE CONTINENT

The great day dawned. It was May 10, not May 8 as originally planned. Torrential rain for two days and the late arrival of T.C. Durant caused the delay.

Facing each other on the track were the Central Pacific's engine *Jupiter*, with a flared funnel stack, and the Union Pacific's engine *No. 119*, with a straight cylindrical stack.

People were everywhere. The air was filled with excitement. Promontory Point was difficult to reach because it was in such a remote place, but there were probably six or seven hundred people attending the ceremony.

Leland Stanford, governor of California, was involved in a freak accident on the way to Promontory Point. A Chinese timber gang was felling trees in the mountains above the railroad track, and a log rolled down the slope on to the rails along which Stanford's train was traveling from California. The engineer braked hard, but could not avoid hitting the log. The cowcatcher was ripped off, but fortunately no one was hurt. The train crawled slowly to the next depot, and another engine was hitched to the carriages. Stanford arrived safely, bringing with him a silver-headed sledgehammer, a polished laurel tie, and four ceremonial spikes: two gold, one silver, and one combination iron, silver and gold.

Another incident involved Thomas C. Durant. As his Union Pacific train pulled into Piedmont, Wyoming, an armed mob of his own tie cutters surrounded his private car and chained the wheels to the rails. The men informed Durant and his startled associates that they had not received any pay since January and intended holding him prisoner until they received their overdue wages. Durant had no choice but to send a telegram to his New York headquarters requesting the payroll fund be telegraphed to him immediately. This was

Success at last! The tracks of the Union Pacific and the Central Pacific Railroads met at Promontory Point on May 10, 1869. When news of the event was flashed across the continent, the whole of the United States celebrated.

done, and Durant and his guests were free to continue their journey. Because Durant was delayed for two days, the ceremony was held over until May 10.

A company of soldiers of the Twenty-first Infantry formed a double line facing the tracks. Officials from both railroads with their families, friends, photographers, reporters, and construction crews all waited for the ceremony to begin at noon. All of the country eagerly awaited the telegraph message that would signal the joining of the continent by iron rails. An iron spike partially driven into a tie was wired up to the national telegraph system. When struck by a hammer the sound would go out over the wires and the whole country would hear it.

The last pair of rails had been laid and the polished laurel tie was slipped beneath the last joint. The four ceremonial spikes were dropped into place, but it was the iron spike that had to be hammered in.

After Stanford and Dodge made their speeches, Stanford, the highest-ranking official present, raised high the heavy silver-headed sledgehammer. A hush fell over the crowd. He brought it smartly down and missed the spike! Durant then took the sledgehammer, swung it, and also missed. So it was the telegraph operator who sent the signal to the waiting country.

The ceremonial spikes and the laurel tie were removed. Cheering workmen clambered up on both engines. Champagne flowed. Everyone milled round excitedly. Reporters were interviewing the officials, the construction bosses, and the workmen. Photographers took pictures of Grenville Dodge, chief engineer of the Union Pacific, shaking hands with Samuel Montague, chief engineer of the Central Pacific.

Then *Jupiter* backed up and made room for *No. 119* to cross the rail junction on to the Central Pacific's tracks. It gave a blast from its whistle as it moved across on to the tracks of the Union Pacific.

After four years the transcontinental railroad had become a reality, and Iron Horses were ready to race across the American continent.

One of the golden spikes used at the ceremony linking the two railroads was inscribed with the following prayer: "May God continue the unity of our country as this railroad unites the two great oceans of the world."

Leland Stanford, the governor of California, who was so proud of the Central Pacific, had had a train named after him some years before the historical birth of the transcontinental railroad. It was the Central Pacific's first locomotive, the wood-burning *Governor Stanford*. When the tracks were laid from Sacramento to Roseville, a distance of 18½ miles, the *Stanford* made its first trip on April 26, 1864, carrying passengers. The fare for one way was $1.85.

THE OPENING UP OF THE WEST

May 10, 1869, was one of the greatest days of the century, but it would be some years before the transcontinental railroad was finally finished.

Tunnels had to be completed and flimsy bridges that were erected during the race across the country had to be securely built. Depots were made into proper stations, around which towns soon sprang up. Thousands of settlers, mainly immigrants from Europe, began to use the railroad to take them to new territory where they could start a new life. Building projects started springing up, and trade began to flourish between the east and west coasts.

The railroads altered the lives of the cowboys. When the Kansas Pacific Railroad started transporting cattle back east, their shipping points were small settlements that grew into notorious cowtowns – Abilene, Ellsworth, and Hays City. Thousands of cattle poured into these towns after long drives up from Texas. The tired and thirsty cowboys needed a place to stay before returning to their ranches, so crude hotels, eating houses, and

William F. Cody killed so many buffalos to provide meat for the Kansas Pacific construction crews, he became world-famous as Buffalo Bill.

saloons sprang up like mushrooms. These cattle drives to the railroad towns were responsible for turning the cowboy into a legendary figure. Before that he was just a stock handler on horseback living on a ranch.

At the end of a drive the cowboys were paid off, and in restless, reckless moods, they spent their wages gambling and drinking. They were rough, tough, and wild and would fight at a drop of a hat, using their fists or more often, their guns. Their shoot-outs brought in sheriffs and marshals and the era of the wild and woolly West began. Without the Iron Horse, such changes could not have taken place.

When the tracks of the Kansas Pacific Railroad reached Fort Riley late in the year of 1866, the glory-seeking Lieutenant Colonel George Armstrong Custer had just arrived to lead the Seventh Cavalry. Their assignment was to keep the Plains Indians away from the railroad.

Working for the Kansas Pacific Railroad was a young man by the name of William F. Cody. He was paid $500 a month to keep the construction crews supplied with buffalo meat. A crack shot with a rifle, he killed so many buffalos that he was nicknamed Buffalo Bill. Without his job with the Kansas Pacific, he might never have become world-famous.

As the building of railroads continued to increase, so fame and fortune was brought to all kinds of people and to all sorts of places. By 1900 there were four more transcontinental railroads across the United States.

THE TRAIN ROBBERS

*I*n the early 1860s, robbing trains was something new to the outlaws who held up stagecoaches and banks.

The first train robbery took place on May 5, 1865, shortly after the end of the Civil War. A band of men, ex-guerrilla fighters of the Civil War, were looking for adventure and easy money. They decided to rob a train owned by

Butch Cassidy, the ruthless bandit who organized the desperate gang known as the Wild Bunch.

the Ohio and Mississippi Railroad. The train was running from St. Louis, Missouri, to Cincinnati, Ohio.

The ruffians derailed the train and as it stopped, they swarmed onto it. Some went through the cars, holding up the passengers at gunpoint and taking all their money and valuables. The rest of the gang robbed the express car of its contents.

Grabbing their loot, they dashed to the river bank where they had moored some skiffs. They managed to escape down the river and were never heard of again. No one ever knew who they were.

The first organized gang of outlaws to stage a train robbery was the Reno Gang. Their first robbery took place near the town of Seymour, Indiana, on October 6, 1866, and was an Adams Express Company train. They got away with $10,000 from the express car.

News of their daring robbery got about and two other outlaws, Walter Hammond and Michael Colleran, decided to follow in the Renos' footsteps. They also robbed an Adams car and got away with $8,000.

The Reno Gang was blamed for the second robbery. They were so angry when they heard about it that they tracked down the offenders and coolly turned them over to the law!

The success of the Reno Gang got the notorious Jesse James and Cole Younger thinking, and they decided to do some train robbing, too. Their first job was a Rock Island and Pacific Railroad train, which they believed was carrying a large shipment of gold from the west coast to Chicago.

On the night of July 21, 1873, they derailed the train a few miles outside the town of Adair, Iowa. But much to their disappointment, the safe in the express car only contained $3,000. After that they pulled off several more successful train robberies, including one near the town of Sedalia, Missouri, when they got away with $14,000. Cole Younger had broken open the safe with a sharp-pointed pick.

It was Butch Cassidy and his Wild Bunch who robbed a Union Pacific train. In the small hours of the morning of June 2, 1899, near Wilcox, Wyoming, the gang flagged down the train. Cassidy and his boys uncoupled the express car and blew it up. Then they dynamited the safe, and the explosion blew thousands of bank notes up in the air. They managed to scoop up $30,000 and made their getaway safely.

The Wild Bunch pulled off three more train robberies and got away with them. When the Pinkerton detectives failed to catch them, the desperate Union Pacific officials offered to pardon Cassidy and give him a job as an express guard.

They promised a good salary, but Butch was not interested. He promptly proceeded to plan another robbery that was also successful. So the Union Pacific decided to form a squad of crack-shot riflemen and put them on a special high-speed train with orders to bring in the Wild Bunch.

But they were too late. Cassidy decided the time had come to leave the country, since things were getting too hot for him. He and the Sundance Kid, Harry Longbaugh, went to South America and carried on with their train robbing activities down there.

Train robbers came up with various ways of stopping trains. They altered the signals, flagged them down, or held them up at water stops. They did not like derailing trains after several accidents had occurred in which people were killed. They did not want to kill anyone, only rob them, and they only shot people who got in their way!

A RAILROAD WAR

For four years a battle raged between the construction crews of the Atchison, Topeka and Sante Fe line and the Denver and Rio Grande railroad. Both were laying tracks south from Colorado into New Mexico in 1876, looking for freight markets.

William Strong was the general manager of the Santa Fe, and William J. Palmer was the founder of the Rio Grande. With both railroads competing with one another, there were bitter fights and a series of lawsuits in the two years it took them to reach Raton Pass, New Mexico.

In 1868, the silver mines at Leadville, Colorado, were producing 100,000 pounds of ore a day. A railroad was desperately needed to transport the silver. The race between the Santa Fe and the Rio Grande to reach Leadville was on.

The only way to reach Leadville was through the Royal Gorge of the Arkansas River. It seemed impossible to build a railroad through it. The cliff walls were 1,000 feet high and they narrowed down to 30 feet in some places, hardly space enough to lay a track. But Strong and Palmer began working their way towards the canyon.

They each got up to some cunning tricks to try to stop the other, including hiring gangs of guerrillas to delay and sabotage each other's work on the tracks. The famous marshal of Dodge City, Bat Masterson, was one of the gunfighters hired by the Santa Fe to protect the crews, while the Rio Grande hired local sheriffs.

Bridges were burned, survey stakes were moved, and road beds were buried under man-made avalanches.

Palmer's graders swam across the Arkansas River and built a crude fort so they could fire on the Santa Fe crews opposite.

Each crew swarmed on the other's trains and captured each other's depots. At one point Palmer's men killed two of Strong's men and wounded two others. Bat Masterson was unable to protect the Santa Fe workmen.

Finally after four years of dirty fighting on both sides, the war came to an end. The men financing the railroads had to stop the costly violence, and in 1880 a compromise was reached.

The Rio Grande got the line to Leadville and agreed to pay the Santa Fe for the track it had

It was the notorious Jesse James gang that derailed a Rock Island and Pacific train on July 21, 1873.

constructed in the gorge. Sante Fe was given the line to El Paso and St. Louis. Later, the Denver and Rio Grande extended to Salt Lake City, where it connected with the Union Pacific. The Atchison, Topeka and Sante Fe eventually extended to California and was to become one of the most profitable railroads in the United States.

But during construction, more violence occurred between these two railroads than between the Union Pacific and Central Pacific during the building of the transcontinental railroad.

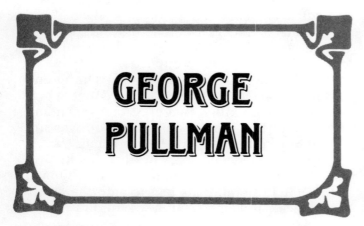

GEORGE PULLMAN

George Pullman never built a railroad, but his name is one of the best known in the history of American railroading.

When people first started traveling by train, the cars were fitted with rows of narrow wooden benches. George Pullman was determined to improve traveling conditions. He wanted passengers to have comfortable seats and berths to sleep in on long journeys.

He managed to persuade the Chicago and Alton railroad to let him have two coaches, and these he turned into crude sleeping cars. All he did was to install hinged upper berths which could be folded up against the car ceiling when not in use, and hinged seats with backs which could be flattened for people to lie back.

The railroad company agreed to try them out on their passengers, and although they were uncomfortable because they were not upholstered, the travelers liked the idea. So Pullman's next step was to upholster the berths, the seats, and the seat backs. From that start, he began designing luxurious sleeping cars with plush seats, fresh linen, and fancy furnishings.

In 1864, he built his own sleeping car, which he named the *Pioneer*. It was roomy and comfortable, but he had made it too wide to go through stations and too high for most bridges. Much to his disappointment no railroad company wanted it. And then, through the tragic assassination of Abraham Lincoln, a use was found for the *Pioneer*.

Because of its roomy interior, it was decided that it would be most suitable to take President Lincoln's coffin to Illinois, where he was to be buried. That meant the stations along the route had to be widened to take the car. This was not such a big problem after all, and so Pullman's car was accepted.

In 1867, he formed the Pullman Palace Car Company, and later he built a huge plant with a town around it, which became known as Pullman, Illinois. Today Pullman is part of Chicago.

In the early days of the railroads there were no dining cars on trains, or any station restaurants west of Topeka. On long journeys trains stopped from time to time to allow cooks to build a fire beside the track and prepare what we call today a barbecue. They cooked buffalo steaks, bacon and other foods. All classes of passengers had their meals out in the open alongside the track.

George Pullman decided something should be done about that, so he built dining cars where passengers could dine in comfort and enjoy delicious meals.

On May 15, 1869, five days after the joining of the rails at Promontory Point, the first transcontinental passenger service was formed. It ran every day. Westbound passengers boarded the Pacific Express at Omaha, bound for Sacramento. Across the continent, eastbound passengers boarded the Atlantic Express at Sacramento, bound for Omaha. It was a 2,000-mile trip and took about four days at a cost of around $100.

Speed and comfort was what travelers wanted, and the wealthy first class passengers got the comfort, thanks to George Pullman's efforts. In addition to his luxurious sleeping and dining cars, there were his magnificent parlor cars. Such luxury is unheard of today in our modern trains.

The poor third-class passengers paid the lowest fare and so had the worst accommodations. They were cowhands, miners, hunters, immigrants, and Indians. But many of them, in later years, made their fortunes out West and no doubt enjoyed the luxuries of first-class travel, thanks to George Pullman.

Bands of outlaw guerrillas were hired by the two railroad companies, the Atchison, Topeka and Santa Fe on one side and the Denver and Rio Grande on the other.

THE RAILROAD HEROES

The real heroes of the railroads were the men who actually built them, the construction crews who with grit and grim determination pitted their lives and skill against high mountains, parched deserts, raging torrents, avalanches, harsh weather conditions, and Indian attacks. It was through their blood, sweat, and unending hard work that the vast United States is now crisscrossed with fine railroads.

Another great transcontinental railway, the Canadian Pacific, spans the east and west coasts of Canada. The intrepid workers who built it suffered the same hardships and shared the same courage as the crews of the American transcontinental railroad.

Built by William Cornelius Van Horne, it was begun in 1881 and finished by 1885. This railroad, too, had to be cut through the Rocky Mountains.

Twelve thousand workers blasted away mountaintops, bored tunnels, drained swamps, and diverted rivers. It was so cold in winter the tracks had to be kept warm to prevent them from cracking. The Canadians were as proud of their transcontinental railroad as the Americans were of theirs, and with just cause. Van Horne loved building railroads. In 1902, he built one in Cuba, and his last project was a railroad in Guatemala in 1908.

One more great railroader must be mentioned. He was James Jerome Hill. Born in 1838, he was a man of lowly beginnings. His business life started in St. Paul, Minnesota, working for various steamship lines. As a young man, still not yet 30 years old, he was selling wood and coal to a Midwestern railroad and at the same time running a small steamship line on the famous Red River, between Minnesota and North Dakota.

He was 40 years old when he and some other rich men, learning that the St. Paul and Pacific railroad was in deep money trouble, took control. Under his clever management, the railroad became a success. From then on, there was no holding back J. J. Hill. He became one of the greatest and most famous railroad empire-builders. He completed the Great Northern railroad in 1893 and shortly afterwards took over the Northern Pacific. He spent the rest of his long life building a railroad empire. When he died in 1916, he left more than $53 million.

Although giant airliners cross the United States and Canada daily and have become the quickest means of travel, they have never totally replaced trains, nor are they likely to.

Trains play a vital part at election time when politicians need them for whistle-stop campaigning. They carry celebrities to outlying areas where normally the residents would be unable to see any famous people in person. They haul heavy freight.

For people who are not in a hurry, travel by rail is leisurely and comfortable. Passengers can view the varied and often breathtaking scenery from the wide windows or from the observation cars.

Trains and aircraft may be in competition, but both are necessary means of transportation. From a train crossing the continent passengers can follow the route taken by courageous pioneers in covered wagons. From an aircraft they can look down with awe and wonder as to how the pioneers ever made their way over such formidable mountain ranges and crossed such wide rivers and empty deserts.

Rail chief Cornelius Van Horne, who was justly proud of achievements not only in Canada but also in Cuba and Guatemala. (Photo: Courtesy Canadian Pacific Archives).

Construction crews not only endured the hardships of the punishing weather but had to be ready at all times for sudden Indian attacks. Many workers died fighting.

GUNFIGHTERS

GUNFIGHTERS

Movies and Western books have gone a long way toward creating myths about the Old West. Most people think that the era of the gunfighters went on for a very long time. In fact, the day of the "shootists" (as they were called in their own time) was very brief. It can be said that the period ran from 1865, the end of the Civil War and the start of the great trail herds, to the late 1880s.

Before the end of the century, progress had overtaken the gunfighter. Outlaws, such as Butch Cassidy and the Sundance Kid, found that their riding days were gone forever. The wide open ranges belonged to the past. Barbed wire fences put an end to bandits on fast horses outgalloping their pursuers across rolling prairies.

Even science conspired against them. The telephone was now in everyday use. That meant that news of a robbery could be transmitted instantly to law officers in the area. Robbers attempting a quick escape were more easily followed and captured.

For a brief period, the gunfighter was king of the Old West. This book relates the deeds of some of the more colorful members.

WILD BILL HICKOK

*J*ames Butler Hickok, to call him by his real name, was born on May 27, 1837, in Homer, Illinois. Homer was later renamed Troy Creek. Hickok was only eighteen when he first ran into trouble. He quarrelled with a teamster and, during the fistfight that followed, they both fell into a canal. Hickok scrambled out safely, but there was no sign of the teamster. Hickok mistakenly believed that the man had drowned and lost no time in leaving the district.

The next time Jim Hickok surfaced, he was in Kansas. It was 1855 and Kansas was a hotbed of treachery and wholesale killing. The seeds of the Civil War were being sown among the pro- and anti-slavery factions. Hickok favored the anti-slavery forces and joined the Free State Army.

In 1861, the Civil War broke out and Hickok left Kansas for Nebraska. He took a job in Rock Creek as a stock tender with the Pony Express and the Overland Express Station. It was at the station that Hickok got into serious trouble with the law.

A farmer named David McCanles and the station manager, Horace Wellman, had argued fiercely about a debt owed to McCanles by the company which owned the Pony Express. McCanles was accompanied by two friends. It was claimed that all three men were unarmed.

Suddenly, the argument erupted into violence. A shot was fired and McCanles fell dead. More shots rang out and his two friends lay dead. Reports differ as to whether it was Hickok or Wellman who fired the shots. Apparently, there was enough suspicion to go around because the sheriff arrested both Hickok and Wellman, together with Wellman's wife and a stable hand named Brink. All four were charged with murder and hauled before the judge. Astonishingly, all four were released on the grounds of self-defense.

With a carving knife and two .36 caliber Navy revolvers, Wild Bill was ready for any sudden attack.

Hickok lost no time hitting the trail out of Rock Creek. Three months afterward, he joined the Union Army as a wagon master.

The Civil War was now raging full force and, once again, it intruded into Hickok's life. He fought in the battle of Wilson's Creek in Missouri. He went on to serve as a scout and spy. It was during this time that he acquired the famous nickname "Wild Bill." Perhaps he earned it because of his daring exploits during the war. Or perhaps Jim was called Wild Bill in contrast to his older brother, Lorenzo, who was known as "Tame Bill."

At the end of the war, Wild Bill was in Springfield, Missouri. He was gambling with a friend named Dave Tutt. There was an argument over a gambling debt. Tutt snatched Hickok's watch from the gambling table, saying that he

would keep it in payment for the money Hickok owed him. Hickok warned Tutt never to use the watch if he valued his life.

Dave Tutt should have known that Hickok would make good his threat. The next day, Tutt displayed the watch in the public square. Wild Bill Hickok was not a man to be mocked. Guns blazed. Tutt missed. Hickok did not.

Wild Bill was charged with murder for the second time. Later, the charge was reduced to manslaughter. Luck was still with him. He was acquitted and released.

Hickok returned briefly to military life. It was during this time he was befriended by the famous Civil War general and frontier fighter, George Armstrong Custer. Custer had heard of Wild Bill's exploits and admired him.

The year 1869 found Hickok, never able to settle down for long, in Hays City, Kansas. At the time, Hays City was crowded with railroad laborers, cowboys, and soldiers from the garrison. Perhaps the law-abiding citizens of Hays City felt the need of a strong, experienced gunman to act as sheriff.

They certainly got experience when they elected Wild Bill sheriff. Soon enough, he was in the thick of the action. On August 24, a man named Bill Melvin and two of his ruffian friends started shooting up the town. Sheriff Hickok shot Melvin dead.

A month later, Hickok was called into a saloon to settle a disturbance. It ended in the death of another man, Sam Strawhun. Saloon patrons grew to be very wary whenever Sheriff Hickok entered.

In July of 1870, Hickok was beaten up in a saloon by some troopers of the 7th Cavalry once commanded by General Custer. Hard hit though he was, Hickok managed to draw his pistol. One trooper dropped in his tracks, dead. Another trooper staggered away, badly wounded.

By now, Wild Bill was ready to pull out of Hays City. He set out for Abilene, Kansas. On April 15, 1871, he was appointed city marshal. Abilene was not any kinder to Bill than Hays City had been.

Phil Coe owned a saloon in town. He was also a gambler and able gunman. A feud developed between the two men. It festered for a while until it finally exploded in gunfire. Hickok mortally wounded Coe. Hearing footsteps behind him, Hickok thought it was one of Coe's friends trying to take him from the back. In a split second, he turned and fired. Horrified, he realized too late that the man he had shot was his good friend and deputy, Mike Williams.

Tired of a life of gunslinging, Wild Bill joined Buffalo Bill Cody's theatrical troupe. Show business wasn't for him, and he soon quit.

One day, he was sitting at a gambling table in Deadwood, South Dakota. He was busy playing cards and didn't notice the young drifter behind him. Jack McCall pulled out his gun and shot Hickok in the back. He was hanged for the cold-blooded murder. He never revealed why he committed the crime. Perhaps he wanted to be the man who shot Wild Bill Hickok.

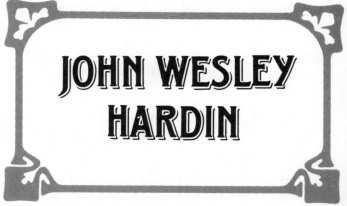

JOHN WESLEY HARDIN

*J*ohn Wesley Hardin was a handsome young man with a steely, relentless gaze. Any gunmen foolish enough to challenge him had only to stare into Hardin's ice-cold eyes glaring across a loaded revolver to know that the sands of time were running out quickly for them.

Strangely enough, this young desperado was named after a man of God. The original John Wesley was the founder of the Methodist religion. That is why, when a son was born to the Reverend and Mrs. J.G. Hardin, they named the boy John Wesley Hardin.

If his parents had hoped that little John would grow up to teach wicked men the error of their ways, as his namesake had done, they were sadly mistaken. The only lesson that many suicidal men facing him learned was that he could draw faster than they could.

Wes Hardin was born on May 26, 1853, in Bonham, Texas. The next twelve years were troubled ones for Texas. Political unrest over the issue of slavery was brewing between the states. The Northern states wanted to free the slaves and the Southern states wanted to retain slavery. A bitter war followed. In 1865 the North won, but savage dislike between the North and South continued.

One day, in the street, twelve-year-old Wes quarrelled with a black boy named Mage. Wes ordered Mage to step aside so that Wes could pass. Mage refused. Harsh words followed and Mage struck at young Hardin with a club. Instantly, Hardin drew a revolver and shot Mage dead.

Wes Hardin fled, pursued by three cavalrymen bent on capturing him. Thinking that he might not be able to outrun them, he waited for them in ambush. Three shots rang out. Three troopers lay dead.

In post-Civil War Texas, shooting a black boy and three Northern soldiers was not considered a crime. Unbelievable as it may seem, Wes Hardin was teaching class in a school in Pisga only a few months later. Pisga was in Novarro County, Texas. His father had recently been appointed head of the school.

By his own account, young Wes was a satisfactory tutor. Wes had two cousins, Tom Dixon and Manning Clements, who later became a well-known rancher. The boys were setting out on the trail one day to round up longhorns. After three months of teaching, Wes decided to join them.

Soon afterward, Wes was accused of another crime. This time, there was no doubt as to his innocence. Even so, he fled, pursued again by Northern troopers. He was overtaken and once more bloodshed followed. Two cavalrymen died under his guns.

John Wesley Hardin was now a very much wanted outlaw. He was only sixteen, but he was reputed to be one of the most dangerous killers in Texas. Now a hunted criminal, he lived a life of constant violence. Murder came easily to him.

In May 1872, he married Jane Bowen, the pretty daughter of a rancher. But his years as an

John Wesley Hardin, the terror of Texas. He feared no man.

outlaw were coming to an end.

With thirty or more killings behind him, John Wesley Hardin shot a man in a saloon. Again he ran, this time to Florida.

He was arrested, tried, and sentenced to twenty-five years in prison. He actually served only fifteen years of his sentence before being released with a full pardon. His wife was now dead, leaving a son and two daughters. Perhaps it was because of them that Hardin decided to stop his life of violence and finally settle down.

It was not to be. His past was too much with him.

It was August, 1895. Hardin was gambling in a saloon in El Paso, Texas. John Sellman, the chief peace officer, entered the saloon. Without a word of explanation, he took out his gun and shot Hardin in the back, killing him.

127

COMMODORE PERRY OWENS

Owens was a tall man with yellow hair, as handsome as a Greek god. He never drank, gambled or smoked, and he had a faultless respect for women. He wore his hair very long.

Commodore Perry Owens's first recorded appearance was as a horse guard at the stage station in Navajo Springs, Arizona. He soon won the grudging respect of the Indians who did their best to run off the horses he was guarding. Once they tried to ambush him. It resulted in four dead Indians. Another story goes that Owens was besieged in the station by more than one hundred Indians. He stood them off for three days until they gave up.

After several years of pointless skirmishes, the Indians finally left him alone.

Life in Arizona in the 1880s was far from peaceful. Troubles erupted between the Americans, the Mexicans, and the Indians. Feuds between families led to all-out warfare.

Pleasant Valley held two such warring families, the Grahams and the Tewksburys. The war began when the Tewksburys drove their sheep into the valley, for cattlemen and sheepherders were bitter enemies.

During this time of turmoil, Navajo County was formed and Holbrook was named as the county capital. Everyone agreed that they needed a sheriff. The position was offered to and accepted by Commodore Perry Owens.

A third family, named Blevins, joined the Pleasant Valley war. Old man Blevins deliberately made an enemy of Owens. It ended in a shootout. The old man and two of his five sons were killed by Owens. The remaining sons joined the Graham family.

War and bloodshed continued until the brutality of the Blevins brothers turned the Grahams against them. In disgust, the Blevins and a notorious rustler named Mose Roberts pulled out and headed for greener pastures. Before leaving, the Blevins brothers decided to visit their mother. Sheriff Owens had warned

Commodore Perry Owens and John Wesley Hardin were similar in three respects. Both were handsome. Both were named after famous men, and both were fast on the draw. In one respect they were not alike. Commodore Perry Owens was a lawman who believed that the law should be respected and obeyed. John Wesley Hardin thought the law was a nuisance and ignored it.

Little is known of Commodore Perry Owens's parents and childhood. His parents must certainly have admired the original Commodore Matthew Galbraith Perry who commanded the U.S. Navy during the latter half of the Mexican War.

Commodore Perry Owens wasted no time when he saw that Andy Blevins was armed.

them to stay away from Holbrook. When news came to him that they were back and uttering threats against him, he quietly loaded his guns and set out.

The Blevins home was crowded that day. With Mrs. Blevins were her three sons, Andy (alias Cooper), the oldest, and the two younger boys, Johnny and Sam. The rustler Roberts (who was also their brother-in-law), the wife of Johnny Blevins, and a Mrs. Gladden and her nine-year-old daughter were also there.

Owens stopped outside the house and called on Andy and his brothers to surrender. Andy appeared, gun in hand. Inside, Johnny, Sam, and Roberts prepared for battle. The fight lasted only a minute, but when Owens rode away unhurt, he left behind him Andy, Sam, and Roberts dead and Johnny badly wounded. The whole of Arizona learned that there was no trifling with Commodore Perry Owens.

He died peacefully in 1919, an honored and highly respected man.

129

CLAY ALLISON

If ever there was a wild one, it was Robert A. Clay Allison. Allison was born in Waynesboro, Wayne County, Tennessee, in 1840. Some people speculate that the irrational behavior he displayed all his life was due to a blow to the head which he received in his childhood.

He was only twenty-one when the Civil War broke out. He enlisted in the Tennessee Light Artillery, fighting for the Southern cause. After only three months of service, he was discharged for his strange behavior. The Confederate army might have figured that it was finished with Clay Allison, but he had not finished with the army. Undaunted, he re-enlisted. This time he chose the cavalry. He fought with them until the end of the war.

After getting out of the army, Allison went to Texas looking for work. He was hired as a trailherder by two famous cattlemen, Oliver

Wyatt Earp and his deputy Bat Masterson were the lawmen of Dodge City.

Loving and Charles Goodnight. Tales of his misdeeds and irresponsible ways began to circulate. As is so often the case with wild men in wild times, rumors flew thick and fast.

A near-explosion occurred in Dodge City, Kansas, when Allison came across Wyatt Earp and Bat Masterson. Earp and Masterson were lawmen in Dodge at the time.

Sure it is that Allison never did like town marshals. He liked them even less if they were Yankees, which both Earp and Masterson were. The very sight of those two stalking the street would have been enough cause for Clay to keep his guns loaded.

Clay Allison, a ruthless gunman with a hair-trigger temper.

That the three men met seems certain. The fact that Allison rode out of town and none of them was wounded would indicate that no gunplay took place. Perhaps Earp and Masterson were not unfriendly toward Clay and sought no quarrel. This may have been one of the few times that Clay was able to keep his temper in check. Lucky it was, too, for when he was aroused he could — and did — kill ruthlessly.

His ever uncertain temper reached fever point when a weeping woman came to Clay and told him that her husband, a rancher named Charles Kennedy, had just killed their infant daughter. The distraught mother went on to tell Allison that her husband was in the habit of murdering any lonely traveler who happened to stop off at the ranch asking for a night's lodging.

This brutal behavior on Kennedy's part infuriated Allison. He gathered some other desperate characters and raced toward the ranch.

Clay Allison was fond of shooting up peaceful towns and scaring the townsfolks.

They awakened the sleeping rancher and hauled him off to jail. Later, some bones were dug up outside the Kennedy cabin. Allison and his gang decided not to wait for a court trial. They stormed the jail, took Kennedy outside, and hanged him.

Normally, Clay Allison did not go out looking for trouble. Left alone, he was a quiet enough man. Every once in a while though, he would start feeling bored. To relieve his pent-up emotions, he would ride through town, guns blazing. It was very dangerous to be on the street when Allison was in town. Even the lawmen didn't try to stop him. It would be like trying to stop a herd of stampeding cattle.

Unlucky was the man against whom he nursed a grievance. There was the time when he rode into Cheyenne with a herd of cattle. He was nursing a painful toothache, and sought out a dentist. By mistake, the dentist pulled the wrong tooth. Furious, Allison found another dentist who removed the right tooth. The crisis over, Allison returned to the first dentist. Hurling the man into a chair, Allison tore a tooth out of the man's jaw and was only prevented from ripping out all his teeth by the arrival of an outraged band of citizens.

Sooner or later, a man with a reputation such as Allison's was bound to meet up with another of the same breed. When that happened it followed that they had to prove who was the better man.

One afternoon Clay Allison was eating in a restaurant seated opposite an ugly customer named Chunk Colbert. Chunk already had seven killings behind him. He did not live long enough to make it eight. Foolishly he slipped his gun out of its holster when he thought Clay was not watching and aimed it under the table. When he fired, the bullet was deflected and missed Allison who did not make the same error. Colbert died and Clay went on quietly with his meal.

In the end, he died at the age of 47 as a result of an accident. He tripped one day, and fell from a wagon he was loading. The nervous horses moved forward, and the wagon ran over Clay, breaking his neck and back.

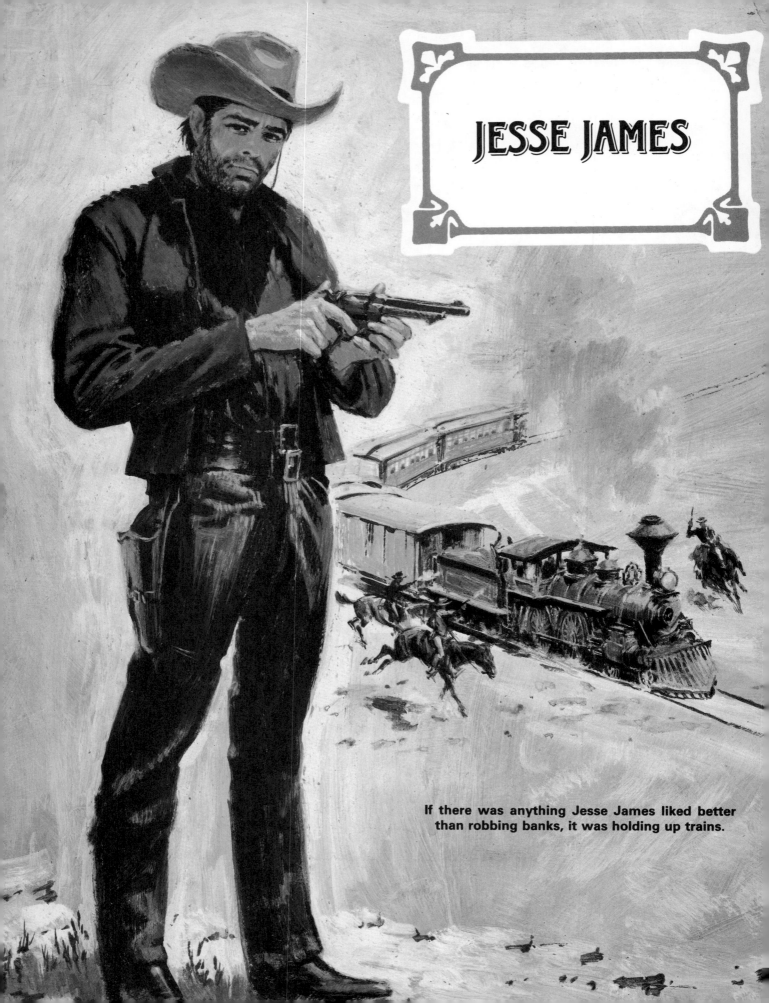

JESSE JAMES

If there was anything Jesse James liked better than robbing banks, it was holding up trains.

esse James was one of two brothers born to Robert and Zerelda James in Clay County, Missouri. His older brother, Alexander Frank, was born in 1843. Jesse was born in 1847. Both brothers earned well deserved reputations as merciless bandits. Jesse was the worse of the two.

At the outbreak of the Civil War in 1861, Frank left home and struck out on his own. By the age of twenty, he was riding with a band of guerrillas led by one of the most blood-thirsty men ever to straddle a saddle. His name was William Clarke Quantrell.

During this time, Jesse stayed home with his mother. His father had died when he was five years old and his mother had married a man named Dr. Reuben Samuel.

One day, several armed men rode up to the Samuel homestead. They said they were looking for Frank. They claimed to be from the Kansas Militia, owing allegiance to the North. When Dr. Samuel told them he did not know Frank's whereabouts, they tortured him. They whipped Jesse and his mother. Having learned nothing, they rode away.

A bitter hatred rose in Jesse's heart as he watched them leave. He vowed to have revenge. Revenge took the form of joining his brother and Quantrell's guerrillas.

It was while Frank and Jesse were members of Quantrell's ruthless gang that they met two other brothers who were to share their future notoriety, Cole and Jim Younger.

To his partners in crime, Jesse was known as "Dingus." The story goes that one day, while practicing his marksmanship, he accidently shot off the top of one of his fingers. "By Dingus! I shot myself!" he yelled. From then on, he was Dingus to all of them.

It was 1865, the last year of the war. Jesse had been shot and badly wounded in one of the gang's raids. He was nursed by his cousin, who bore the same first name as his mother, Zerelda Mimms. Jesse never forgot Zerelda's care and attention. Ten years later they were married.

Those were bad days for the people of Missouri. They had sided with the South in the war and the South had lost. In punishment, they were attacked and driven from their homes. There was much bitterness toward Northerners and much admiration for anyone who would fight back against the Northerners. That is why the James and Younger brothers, outlaws though they were, could find help and shelter from the law.

Jesse James was known to all his friends as Dingus.

By this time, Jesse and Frank had been fighting and raiding for too long ever to settle down to peaceful lives. They were used to being outlaws. Two other Younger brothers, Bob and John, joined the gang.

In May of 1865, a month after the war ended, Quantrell was ambushed by Union soldiers and killed. Nine months later, Jesse led a band of raiders into the town of Liberty, Missouri. Guns blazing, they smashed their way into the First National Bank and made off with $15,000 in gold coins. As they rode away, they killed a young college student who was standing in the street.

This was the first bank robbery to take place in the United States. It created a sensation. Triumphantly, Jesse planned fresh raids. Lexington, Missouri, and Richmond, Missouri,

135

were pinpointed as future targets. Soon their safes were emptied under the threatening guns of the James/Younger gang.

For several years, the gang continued to rob banks throughout Missouri. Then, on July 23, 1873, they changed their tactics.

They robbed a train in Iowa. Disappointed, they rode off with only $7,000. Later they found out that they had robbed the wrong train. Quick to correct their error, they headed for the Gads Hill depot in Missouri to wait for the arrival of the Iron Mountain Express. To be sure that there was no interference, they herded all the honest citizens into the depot building. With no one to stop them, they held up the train and made a clean getaway.

They might not have realized it, but time was running out for the James/Younger gang. The famous Pinkerton Detective Agency was put on their trail. Soon afterward, John Younger was killed by a Pinkerton man.

It was in Northfield, Minnesota, that the James and Younger brothers rode together for the last time. On one of their raids, the local residents fought back. Two outlaws, Clell Miller and Bill Chadwell, were shot dead. Jim, Bob, and Cole Younger were wounded and rounded up two weeks later.

Frank and Jesse managed to escape. Both went into hiding. Jesse went to live with his wife and two children.

Still eager for action, Jesse planned a new robbery. He enlisted the aid of his two cousins, Bob and Charlie Ford. Now there was a price on his head: $25,000 reward for the death or capture of Jesse James. All that money was just too tempting for Bob Ford. Jesse James, probably the best known of all the Western outlaws, was shot in the back of the head while hanging a picture on his bedroom wall.

In 1882, the same year Jesse died, Frank James surrendered to the law. He served time in prison and died a free man in February, 1915.

Jesse should have known better than to take off his guns and turn his back on an armed man.

BILLY THE KID

Billy the Kid's days as a gunfighter began in the little township of Lincoln County, New Mexico, in 1877. He drifted into town alone, looking for a job. For some unknown reason, an English rancher and storeowner named John Tunstall took a liking to him and hired him as a ranch hand.

Billy's past was murky, to say the least. There are few reliable facts. It was said that his father died when Billy was very young. He and his widowed mother drifted from town to town and state to state until finally settling in Silver City, New Mexico.

In Santa Fe on March 1, 1873, Billy's mother married a former private in the Indiana Volunteer Infantry. His name was William H. Antrim. Billy's real name was Henry, so for some time he was known as Henry Antrim.

Billy was about fifteen when his mother died. Soon after that, he started to get into trouble. He was accused of helping a no-good character named Sombrero Jack to steal some clothes from two Chinese people. He was arrested and thrown in jail. Somehow he managed to escape and fled to Arizona.

Known as Kid Antrim, he worked on a ranch. It was at this time that Billy killed his first man. The man, E.P. Cahill, was a bully who thought that the undersized whelp would be easily cowed. He was wrong. A bitter quarrel ensued. Then came a fistfight. Billy was knocked to the ground. He saw Cahill coming at him again. Quickly, he whipped out his gun and shot Cahill dead.

Billy was arrested again, this time for murder. True to form, again he escaped from jail. He bolted to Lincoln, New Mexico, and it was there that he was called Billy the Kid and met John Tunstall. Tunstall was in a tough situation. Rashly, he had opened a store in Lincoln. He took as his partner a lawyer named Alexander McSween. A competitive store in town was run by three crafty, ruthless men named Laurence G. Murphy, James J. Dolan, and John H. Riley. They were involved in cattle rustling and shady political activities. They were not standing for competition from an Englishman and a slick lawyer.

On the trumped-up charge of an unpaid debt, they laid claim to some of Tunstall's horses. They sent men to round up the horses.

This young man was known by many names but it was as Billy the Kid that he was known throughout the United States.

John Tunstall tried to stop them. He was shot dead in cold blood. Watching all this was an undersized, buck-toothed rider called Billy.

Billy escaped and swore revenge. A posse was formed to capture the killers. Two were taken into custody. Billy shot both of them.

One killing followed another as the feud continued. One night Billy and several other Tunstall/McSween followers were trapped in McSween's house by their enemies. The house was set on fire. Billy begged McSween and his wife to make a break for it. Billy loaded his guns. McSween led the way and was shot dead. Behind him, Billy herded the others out of the burning building. Harvey Morris, a law student working in McSween's office, was then killed, but all the others escaped.

By now, there had been so many men killed on both sides in Lincoln, the dispute had become known as the Lincoln County War. At this time, a new governor of New Mexico was elected. He was a former major general in the Civil War. His name was Lew Wallace, the author of the novel *Ben Hur*.

Wallace tried to bring peace to Lincoln County. One of his first acts was to send word to Billy the Kid that the governor would guarantee his safety, if he surrendered.

Billy accepted the governor's promise. He turned himself in and handed over his guns. Unfortunately, the District Attorney, William R. Rynerson, was a friend of Billy's enemies. He ignored the governor's pardon and tried to prosecute Billy anyway.

Once again, Billy broke out of jail. This is one of the few times in Billy's life that the records as to his whereabouts are precise. On January 10, 1880, Billy showed up in a saloon in Fort Sumner, New Mexico. Wherever the Kid went, there was trouble. A brawl led to a gunfight, and another man lay dead at Billy's feet.

Later that year, a peace officer named Pat Garrett drifted into Lincoln. He was a tall and deliberate man. His mission was to catch Billy. Twice Garrett cornered the Kid, leaving bloodshed behind. Finally, in December 1880, Garrett captured the Kid.

Billy was taken to Mesilla, New Mexico. There he stood trial for the murder of Sheriff Brady, who had been ambushed and shot not long after the Tunstall killing. Although there was no actual proof that Billy had committed the murder, he was sentenced to death and taken to Lincoln to be hanged.

The rope was never braided that would hang Billy the Kid. One day, he killed his two guards and made his last escape.

Three months later, word reached Pat Garrett that Billy was hiding in Fort Sumner. Garrett went there and hid in the house of Pete Maxwell, an informer against Billy. At midnight, Billy crept into the house. In the darkness, he did not see Garrett, but Garrett saw him. He was not about to give Billy the Kid another chance to escape. He shot the Kid right through the heart.

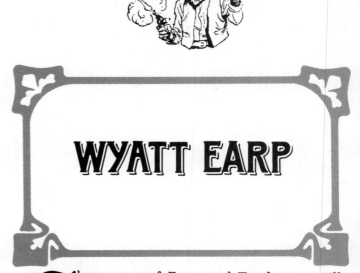

WYATT EARP

The names of Earp and Tombstone will be linked forever. It was in the town of Tombstone in October, 1881, that three Earp brothers with their friend, Doc Holliday, headed toward the O.K. Corral for a showdown with their sworn enemies, the Clanton brothers and the McLaury brothers.

As is so often the case, the golden-haired superman of legend is quite different from the real man. So it is with Wyatt Earp.

His full name was Wyatt Berry Stapp Earp. He was born in 1848 in Monmouth, Illinois. First he tried his hand on the right side of the law. In 1870, he was elected a peace officer in Lamar County, Missouri. He did not find life as a lawman interesting enough to detain him for long.

In 1871, he was arrested for horse stealing in Oklahoma. He paid a bail of $500 and fled the territory before being brought to trial. In 1874, he was in Wichita, again serving as a lawman. This spell of honesty did not last long, however. Soon he was in trouble for refusing to turn over fines he had collected from lawbreakers. Again Earp was forced to hit the road.

The years 1876 to 1879 found him in Dodge City, Kansas. There he balanced two conflicting professions, assistant marshal and professional gambler. You might say that he had it both ways — nobody was ever going to accuse the deputy marshal of cheating at cards.

Alongside Wyatt Earp in Dodge City was his Indian-fighter friend, Bat Masterson. Despite Earp's lawless tendencies, he managed to keep everyone else in line. In fact, Earp and Masterson earned a reputation for being tough on lawbreakers. Earp was quick on the draw and took no nonsense from anyone.

In December 1879, Wyatt and his two

Any man who drew a gun in a Dodge City saloon was very close to certain death if Wyatt Earp happened to be present.

brothers, Morgan and Virgil, arrived in Tombstone, Cochise County, Arizona. The town had been named by Ed Schieffelin, a prospector who had discovered a rich silver lode there. After a lucky strike, he named his diggings Tombstone. It was a rough town and Earp had been warned that all he was likely to find there was a tombstone.

Cochise County was one of the most lawless areas in the West. Roughnecks and killers robbed stages, rustled cattle, and terrorized law-abiding citizens.

Virgil Earp was appointed town marshal of Tombstone. From time to time, his brothers Wyatt and Morgan acted as his deputies. Two years after the Earps hit town, the governor of Arizona reported to the Secretary of State that much of the blame for the continued lawlessness in Tombstone could be leveled at the local peace officers.

The governor visited Tombstone and talked with the county sheriff, John Behan. Behan complained that Virgil Earp was not cooperating with him in bringing the wrongdoers to justice. Virgil made the same complaint against Behan.

Trouble was boiling and the Earps readied themselves for gunplay. A friend of theirs had recently joined them in Tombstone. His name

Wyatt Earp whose name will always be linked with the gunfight at the O.K. corral.

was John Holliday. He was a gambling dentist, who spent more time drawing aces than pulling teeth. He was well known throughout the West by his nickname, "Doc." Doc was a skillful gunman and a valuable ally in any gunfight.

On October 26, 1881, an armed group of rustlers, the Clantons and the McLaurys, arrived in Tombstone. They had known the Earps in another town and had quarrelled bitterly with them.

The Earps and Doc Holliday set out to arrest these rustlers. Sheriff Behan attempted to stop them, but they brushed him aside. A short, but deadly, gunfight took place. It has gone down in history as the "Gunfight at the O.K. Corral." In fact, it took place on the street some distance from the corral. In less than a minute both McLaurys and Billy Clanton were dead. Doc Holliday, Virgil, and Morgan Earp were wounded. Only Ike Clanton and Wyatt Earp survived the fight without a scratch.

Despite his lawless ways, Wyatt Earp died peacefully in bed in 1929.

Butch Cassidy knew that some day he might like to take a trip abroad. Cassidy was not a man to save up for such things, as a normal person would. No, he was always attracted to the lawless approach.

With the aid of several other outlaws, he held up a train. It was a successful raid — or so it seemed at the time. There was just one difficulty; although the take amounted to some $65,000 in currency, all the bills were new and not one of them had been signed officially by the bank!

They were worthless. If Butch Cassidy had been a better student, this incident might have taught him something about the pointlessness of leading a life of crime. Unfortunately, Butch had to learn his lessons the hard way.

Cassidy was one of the leading members in a gang of outlaws called "The Wild Bunch," a name given to them by the newspapers in the

THE WILD BUNCH

The Wild Bunch were wanted for holding up trains but they were not always as successful as they wished.

area they were rustling. They were also known as "The Long Riders" and "The Hole in the Wall Gang." This last name came from the Hole in the Wall Valley, which was one of the places at which they gathered before a robbery.

Nicknames were commonplace among the Wild Bunch. "Butch Cassidy's" real name was Robert Leroy Parker. Harry Longbaugh was known as the "Sundance Kid." Ben Kilpatrick was referred to as the "Tall Texan." George Curry was "Flatnose," for an obvious reason. Hard-of-hearing Camillo Hanks was called "Deaf Charlie."

When Butch was a boy in Beaver, Utah, he had been friends with a rustler named Mike Cassidy. Searching for a man to look up to, young Butch latched on to Mike. Not only did he take Cassidy's name, but he adopted his profession and learned from him the ways to steal horses and rustle cattle.

Butch started out as a horse thief. In 1894, he was caught and sentenced to two years in prison for horse stealing. He was released in 1896 and was fortunate never to see the inside of a prison again.

Even before his imprisonment, Butch had branched out into other areas of crime. On July 24, 1889, he robbed his first bank. With help from Matt Warner and two brothers named Bill and Tom McCarty, he raided the San Miguel Valley Bank in Colorado and made a clean get-away. No one was hurt.

Butch was a thief and guns were the tools of his trade. But, to give him his due, he never killed anyone. He would shoot the horse of anyone chasing him, not the rider.

That could not be said of some of the other members of the gang, however. His sidekick, the Sundance Kid, was certainly a killer. The worst of them all, though, was a cold-blooded outlaw who called himself Kid Curry. He had been a friend of Flatnose George Curry and, like Butch, he had adopted the name of his hero. His real name was Harvey Logan.

The Wild Bunch staged a robbery at a bank in Montpelier, Idaho. Soon afterward, Butch and Elza Lay, (also known as William McGinniss) another member of the gang, brought off another daring robbery. Disguising themselves as miners, they surprised the paymaster at the Castle Gate mine in Utah by thrusting a pistol in his face and demanding the money from the safe. Encouraged by these successes, they robbed a bank in Belle

Fourche, South Dakota. This time they galloped away with $30,000.

With success came unwanted fame. The Wild Bunch was too well known for its own good. Most of the lawmen in the country wanted the glory of capturing them. They even attracted the attention of the famous Pinkerton Detective Agency.

Hoping to take the heat off, The Wild Bunch split up for a time. Butch and Elza Lay went to Alma, New Mexico, where they worked as cowhands for the WS Ranch.

Going straight was hard on Lay. He was captured during a train robbery and sent to prison for life.

In 1899, The Wild Bunch was back in business. They stopped the Union Pacific's Overland Limited and got away with $30,000.

One daring raid followed another. Boldly, they even stopped to have their picture taken after a bank robbery. They sent a copy of it back to the bank with thanks for the contribution to their funds!

It was at this time that Butch decided it would be a good idea to leave the country. That was when he stole the $65,000 in unsigned bills.

Eight years and several bank and train robberies later, Butch and the Sundance Kid found themselves in the country of Bolivia in South America. One rumor has it that they were killed in Bolivia by soldiers. Another claim is that Butch somehow escaped the law in Bolivia and returned safely to the United States.

As for the rest of The Wild Bunch, some were killed and some, like Kid Curry, just plain disappeared. One story goes that Kid Curry was hotly pursued by lawmen after a train robbery in Colorado. Trapped, and not wanting to be taken alive, he committed suicide.

The photograph that the gang sent to a bank they had robbed. With it, went a note of thanks. Left to right, standing, are Bill Carver and Harry "Kid" Logan. Seated are Harry "Sundance Kid" Longbaugh, Ben Kilpatrick and Butch Cassidy.

GUNS OF THE GUNFIGHTERS

"No law west of the Mississippi, no God west of the Pecos."

So went the old saying. Life was cheap in the Old West. Lawlessness prevailed. Honest citizens knew that they had to be prepared to defend themselves at any time. Most people carried their guns with them as a normal part of their everyday dress. Guns were easy to obtain. A Colt .45 could be bought by mail order for seventeen dollars.

Men who were labelled "gunfighters" could be

The best-selling rifle in the West, the Winchester .44-.40. This 1873 model has an extra rear sight for greater accuracy.

on either side of the law. Some — like Wyatt Earp — tried both sides to see which one was more profitable.

Motion pictures have generally given us an unrealistic view of the Old West. A case in point is the two man gunfight. The classic scene goes like this: two men walk toward each other on a dusty street. The hero waits for the bad guy to draw first and only then does he fire. Such chivalrous behavior would more than likely have resulted in the hero lying dead at the feet of his jubilant killer.

Another false idea is that of the quick-draw dead shot. It was Wild Bill Hickok, a man who never took chances, who said: "Whenever you get into a quarrel be sure and not shoot too quick. I've known many a fellar slip up for shooting in a hurry."

A gunman had to be a real wizard to be both fast and accurate. For one thing, many guns were not accurate when they were fired. Misfires were common, especially with percussion revolvers. Even if a man was fast on the draw, his gun might fail him.

The Remington "Over-and-Under" 0.41, 2-shot model. Over 150,000 were sold.

It was Samuel Colt who was responsible for the most popular revolvers produced during the lawless era of the Old West. He did not invent the revolver; he redesigned the action.

His first two guns were only moderately successful. His first revolver fired six .44 caliber shots instead of the customary five. It was too heavy; it weighed more than four pounds. His next produc-

The Colt .45 of 1873 was, without doubt, the most famous revolver of all time.

tion was the Dragoon or Army revolver which came out in 1848. It was lighter than the first weapon, but still unsatisfactory. It remained in production for only fifteen years.

In 1851, Colt finally got it right. His .36 caliber Navy revolver established Sam Colt's reputation as a master gunmaker. One photograph shows Wild Bill Hickok with two such revolvers in his belt.

In 1873, the Single-Action Army Colt revolver was produced. It was known in western folklore as the "Peacemaker." It became the gunfighters' favorite handgun and is still on sale today.

One of the most colorful Frontier characters active in the pursuit of many notorious outlaws was Charles A. Siringo. He was one of the ace detectives on the Pinkerton payroll.

Charlie Siringo was noted for his gun-play. His favorite guns were the Winchester '73 and the Colt .45. First he used the .44 Henry rimfire caliber Winchester '66 and then the famous .44-40 Model '73. This was the rifle that was called "The Gun That Won the West."

It is often stated that the Colt and the Winchester were the gunfighters' most popular weapons. Of course, there were other gunmakers. Remington and another company, Smith and Wesson, also produced splendid guns. So did the U.S. Government armory at Springfield, Massachusetts.

Last, but by no means least, were the shotguns which were devastating firearms. It is sufficient to say that Doc Holliday's enemies could testify to his marksmanship. He used what he called his "street howitzer," a 10-gauge double shotgun. Remington and Winchester specialized in these destructive guns.

SOLDIERS

SOLDIERS

When the Indians of the American West went on the warpath against the white men, the task of subduing the warring tribes fell to the United States Army. The role of the soldiers was similar to that of a police force. They were to protect the white settlers and try to bring about a peace between the white pioneers and the Indians.

At first, however, the soldiers were not prepared for the entirely new way of fighting that faced them. They were used to fighting against men who were trained in regular army warfare. Their new enemies were tough, ferocious guerrilla fighters who swooped down on settlements in lightning raids, burning and killing. They appeared suddenly out of nowhere to attack wagon trains and stage-coaches. They had mastered the art of hit-and-run tactics. Being superb horsemen, they made their getaway at speed, leaving lookouts posted along their trail to deal with any pursuing soldiers. They broke up into small parties, covering their tracks so thoroughly that cavalry detachments frequently found the chase hopeless.

When the American Civil War between the North and South ended in 1865, the United States Army was greatly reduced in numbers. As a result, the soldiers who fought in the Indian wars often found themselves outnumbered and up against appalling odds.

In the end, though, they defeated the Indians in December 1890. The victorious army had complete control over the West, and the defeated Indians lost their freedom, their lands, and their way of life.

The story that follows relates to some of the United States Army's battles against its daunting Native American enemies.

TREACHERY IN APACHE PASS

Second Lieutenant George N. Bascom rode at the head of a platoon of infantry who were mounted on mules. As he headed for Apache Pass in the Dragoon Mountains in Arizona, he knew little of what was to come. Within a short time, he would be responsible for starting a terrible war of vengeance and bloodshed. It was to last for eleven years and would cost the Americans hundreds of lives.

George Bascom was a young, inexperienced officer. He was fresh from West Point Military Academy, and he knew nothing about Indians. He did not know the difference between an outlaw Indian and a chieftain. To him all Indians were alike. He was soon to learn differently.

Cochise was Chief of the Chiricahua (Cheer-a-KA-wa) Apaches. He was an intelligent and wise leader, and a strong, powerfully built man. He was friendly with the whites who came to his territory, and those who knew him respected and liked him. Cochise allowed them to run a stagecoach line through Apache Pass. To protect the stagecoaches his warriors guarded the pass against renegade Apache bands who were not of his tribe. He also supplied wood for the stage station in the middle of the pass.

This was the peaceful situation between Cochise and the whites until January 1861, when Bascom was sent to question Cochise

Lieutenant Bascomb led his men through Apache Pass watched by Apache scouts.

about the kidnapping of a white boy.

A renegade band of Apaches had raided a ranch belonging to a settler named John Ward. They had run off with his cattle and had also taken his stepson. Ward reported the incident to the commanding officer of the nearest army post. He blamed Cochise, whom he did not know, for the raid, because he knew Cochise's warriors were in the area. The fort commander tried to convince Ward that Cochise was peaceful and friendly and would not have done such a thing. But Ward would not listen, and he insisted that the Apache chief be brought in for questioning. Had a more experienced officer, instead of Bascom, been sent to bring Cochise in, the history of Arizona might well have been very different.

Lieutenant Bascom went straight through Apache Pass. That showed how inexperienced he was, because if Cochise had been responsible for the raid on Ward's ranch, it would have meant that he was hostile. And if he were hostile, he could easily have attacked Bascom in the pass. Bascom believed him to be hostile, yet he led his men into the pass without first sending out scouts to make sure it was safe. The pass was a deep, narrow canyon through the mountains, a real deathtrap where hostile Apaches could have wiped out his force in a matter of minutes. Luckily for him and his platoon, Cochise was friendly. Bascom and his men rode safely through to the stage station.

The stationmaster did his best to make Bascom realize he was making a big mistake in assuming that Cochise was guilty of the raid. But Bascom preferred to accept Ward's accusation.

Cochise was invited to Bascom's tent under a white flag of peace. He took several of his people with him. Through an interpreter, Bascom accused Cochise of raiding Ward's ranch and demanded the return of the boy and the cattle.

The Apache chief realized that the young officer had much to learn. Through the interpreter, Cochise told Bascom that because he was new to Apache country and did not understand the ways of his people, he would overlook the insult of accusing him of the raid. He offered Bascom his hand in friendship and said he would find out which Apache band had stolen the boy and the cattle. Cochise promised he would do all he could to see that they were returned to Ward.

Bascom was furious that Cochise had dared to speak to him as an equal. Angrily he told the chief that he would hold him and his companions prisoner until the Ward boy was found. Ordering his sergeant to arrest the Apaches, he turned his back on Cochise and stalked out of the tent.

A sudden, dangerous glint shone in the eyes of Cochise, and a look of pure hatred spread across his handsome face. No man insulted the chief of the Chiricahua Apaches.

In a lightning move he whipped out his knife, slashed the back of the tent and escaped before the startled soldiers standing outside realized what was happening. By the time they fired after him he was well away. A stray bullet hit him in the leg, but he managed to reach the rocky path leading up to his camp.

Bascom, now more angry than ever over the escape of Cochise, gave orders for the other Apaches to be taken prisoner.

APACHE VENGEANCE

Most of the infantrymen under Bascom's command were worried at his treatment of Cochise. His sergeant warned him that a full-scale war could follow if he did not release the remaining Apaches. Bascom's pride though, would not let him take the advice of men more experienced in the ways of the Apaches, and he refused.

Cochise, in his anger, called the entire Apache nation to war. He told the chiefs of the other Apache tribes that the days of friendship with the whites had ended because of the treachery of the lieutenant.

He captured three whites and held them hostage. He offered to exchange them for the Apaches who were being held prisoner, but Bascom would not agree. He told Cochise to return the Ward boy. Only then would Bascom release the Apaches.

Cochise's warriors lost no time in going on

Lieutenant George N. Bascomb

the warpath. They attacked a stagecoach and killed the teamsters. Then they ran off a herd of cattle being watered at a spring near the stage station, killing a white man and wounding two more. During this attack some Indians were killed.

The deaths of his warriors aroused the fury of Cochise even more, and he killed the three white men he had been holding hostage, together with the stationmaster.

In retaliation, the Apaches held by Bascom were hanged. Cochise assumed that it was the lieutenant who gave the order to hang them. In fact it was not Bascom, but a Doctor Irwin, who had brought medical supplies to Bascom's camp. Bascom had protested against the hanging. He was beginning to realize that an Indian uprising was about to take place.

In the years that followed, Cochise waged a relentless battle against the whites in Arizona, New Mexico, and across the border into Mexico. Many hundreds of soldiers and settlers were killed.

The United States Army sent thousands of soldiers, infantry, and cavalry to the Southwest to try to capture Cochise. The troops were load-

ed down with equipment, food, and supplies. They were no match for the Apaches who made lightning attacks then rapidly disappeared into the rocky wilderness of the mountains, leaving no trails behind them. To confuse the soldiers, they attacked in several places at the same time.

The Apaches were living up to their name, which means "enemy." The army had never come up against such a cunning and deadly foe.

The U.S. government was alarmed, because the Apaches were having everything their own way. Some of the finest, most courageous officers, who thought they knew the ways of Indian fighting, were powerless to stop the warring Apaches. Government troops were continually on the move but were unable to make any headway. They tried many times to get Cochise to come to terms, but he refused to meet any high-ranking officers. After the behavior of Bascom, he suspected treachery and no longer trusted them.

THE WAR DRUMS CEASE

*P*resident Grant gave General O.O. Howard the job of trying to find a peaceful solution to the Indian problems of the Southwest.

It was a good move. General Howard was a fine man. He felt sorry for the Indian tribes, who had been so disgracefully treated by his government. He wanted more than anything to end the terrible war between his people and the Apaches. He felt that if only he could talk to Cochise, the chief might be willing to come to terms.

Reaching Cochise was the problem. Luck, however, was with Howard. In New Mexico he met a white man, Tom Jeffords, who was not only a friend of Cochise but was his blood-brother. General Howard explained to Jeffords

that it was his job to end the bloodshed that had lasted for eleven years. Would Jeffords take him to Cochise so that he could talk to him?

Jeffords agreed but he could only guarantee Howard's safety if he would go with him alone. Cochise would not let the general into his stronghold if he had soldiers with him.

Howard trusted Jeffords and promised to leave his army escort behind. They set off to journey the several hundred miles to Arizona with two Apache guides, friends of Jeffords. One was a nephew of Cochise, and the other was the son of an old friend of the chief. On reaching Arizona, the guides sent up smoke

Tom Jeffords was not only a friend of Cochise, the Apache chieftain, he was also the Indian's blood-brother. Tom knew he would be welcome in Cochise's camp.

signals to warn all Apaches that the four men were headed for Cochise's stronghold and were friends.

Arriving at last in the foothills of the Dragoon Mountains, they were met by two of Cochise's warriors and escorted to his camp high up in the mountains.

General Howard waited patiently while Jeffords and Cochise greeted each other. After the greetings were over, Jeffords, who spoke the Apache language, introduced Cochise to Howard, telling him he could trust the general who had been sent by the Great Father in Washington to make peace between the Apaches and the white people.

A warm smile touched Cochise's mouth as he shook hands with the general and welcomed him to his lodge.

As Howard looked at the friendly, open-faced man before him, he found it hard to connect him with all the terrible Apache raids. He saw a man of intelligence and strong character, not a savage. Howard could not help but like Cochise.

Cochise admitted that he wanted peace more than anything, and that it was not he who had broken it in the first place.

Howard assured the chieftain that this time the President of the United States really wished to have a lasting peace with the Chiricahua Apaches.

After a lot of discussion, Cochise came to terms with the general. There would be no more fighting on either side. He insisted that the Chiricahua reservation should include the mountains and valleys of his tribe's homeland. Any other climate might affect the health of his people and eventually kill them, and he would not allow that to happen. He also insisted that Tom Jeffords be appointed the Apache Indian Agent. Jeffords did not want the job, but he could not let his friend down. For the sake of peace, he reluctantly agreed.

General Howard happily agreed to the Chief's reasonable demands. He had done what he had set out to do; he had ended the long Apache war.

Cochise kept the terms of peace until his death on June 8, 1874.

As for Lieutenant Bascom, he was killed a year after his meeting with Cochise. He died, not at the hands of Apaches, but during a battle in New Mexico between the Union and Confederate troops. The Civil War had spread to the Southwest.

Mickey Free, the army scout.

THE KIDNAPPED BOY

The boy who was kidnapped by a band of Apaches was never returned to his stepfather, John Ward. His name was Felix Telles, and he was about twelve years old when he was snatched from his home. He spent his boyhood with the Apaches. Eventually he gained his freedom and became an army scout. For some unknown reason, he decided to use the name Mickey Free.

Because his kidnapping had led to eleven years of war between the whites and the Apaches, he was blamed and hated by the Indians. Such feelings were unfair on the part of the Apaches, because it was not the boy's fault that he had been kidnapped and that war had resulted.

The feeling was mutual, though. Mickey hated the Apaches, and it is said that he did all he could to stir up trouble for them. Because he could speak English as well as Apache, he was used as an army interpreter until the chiefs found out that he was twisting their words, making it impossible at times for them to reach terms. Once they discovered his treachery they refused to speak through him and insisted on their own interpreters.

Although the whites found him reliable, not many of the army scouts liked him any more than the Apaches did.

It would seem that Mickey Free did not have a happy life.

The year was 1868 and the frontier was in the grip of a vengeance war. Several battles took place between Indians and the U.S. Cavalry.

THE VALIANT VOLUNTEERS

General Philip Sheridan was frustrated and angered by the guerrilla tactics of the Plains Indians.

It was 1868 and the frontier was in the grip of a vengeance war. The Cheyennes and their allies, the Sioux and the Arapahos, were on the rampage, killing, raiding, and plundering. No army patrol, no homestead, no white settlement was safe from the fury of the warriors.

General Sheridan was in charge of the Indian campaign that covered more than a million square miles of frontier country. This area was the home of some 192,000 Indians. Sheridan

was worried, because he had an insufficient number of trained soldiers to hold the Indians in check. Seventy-six army posts and camps were spread over the territory, but Sheridan needed more cavalry and infantry regiments to man the garrisons. Only if he got these men could he hope to subdue the warriors of the ninety-nine tribes who were on the warpath.

The General's aide-de-camp, Major George Forsyth, known to his fellow officers as Sandy, suggested a solution.

He believed that the army had been using the wrong tactics to fight the Indians. He thought that a small, highly mobile force of men who traveled light and fast would be far more effective than large forces of troops slowed down by cumbersome supply wagons. These small forces could track down the Indians and make them fight.

Sandy Forsyth had risen from a private of dragoons to brevet brigadier general in the Civil War. He was the trusted aide of General Sheridan, the Union Army Cavalry hero. At the end of the war Forsyth had willingly given up his high rank and reverted back to major in order to join the Indian-Fighting Army and be again under the command of Sheridan.

Major Sandy Forsyth gathered together a troop of fifty tough volunteers, mostly veterans of the Civil War.

General Sheridan knew of Forsyth's distinguished gallantry during the war and considered him an excellent officer. General Sheridan was impressed by his suggestion and told him to organize a troop of fifty volunteers without delay.

Major Forsyth quickly gathered his troop of volunteers together. His second in command was First Lieutenant Fred H. Beecher. Another soldier, General William H.H. McCall, was so anxious to see action that he took the much-reduced rank of sergeant in order to ride with Forsyth. All fifty volunteers were men of outstanding courage, mostly veterans of the Civil War. They were ready and willing to risk their lives in subduing the warring Indians.

Early one morning in late August of 1868, the intrepid little troop rode out from Fort Hayes, complete with a pack train of four mules carrying ammunition and medical supplies. Each man was armed with a seven shot Spencer repeating rifle and an army model Colt revolver. They were on the track of

a band of Indians who had attacked a freight wagon near the western terminus of the Kansas Pacific railroad. The wagon drivers had been killed in the attack.

During the days of hard riding that followed, Forsyth and his men kept losing and then picking up the trail of a fairly large war party. The trail eventually brought them close to the favorite camping grounds of the Cheyenne, Sioux, and Arapahos in Colorado.

On the afternoon of September 16, their scout, Abner "Sharp" Grover, spotted recent tracks of another large band of warriors in a valley at the fork of the Arikaree and Republican Rivers. These warriors appeared to have joined forces with the war party Forsyth and his men had been trailing.

The Major decided that the valley was a good spot to make camp since there was a small brush-covered island in the middle of the river bed that would provide an excellent defensive position if it were needed. He planned to rest that night and attack the warriors' camp the next morning. He knew that Indians seldom attacked at night and did not think that he and his men had been detected by the Indians, but he took no chances. He posted sentries, had the

The alarm was raised at dawn and the sleeping soldiers were soon roused. Quickly they grabbed their guns.

men tether their horses and pack mules securely, and told them to keep their rifles beside them when they bedded down.

But the Indians had spotted them. At dawn the following day, 600 war-painted warriors were poised on the hills overlooking the soldiers' camp, ready to attack.

Fortunately for Forsyth and his men, the surprise attack was spoiled by some overeager young warriors who swooped down on the camp uttering hideous war cries in an attempt to stampede the soldiers' horses. Their attempt failed, since the mounts had been securely tethered, and the sentries managed to turn them back. The noise roused the camp, and the soldiers hurriedly saddled their mounts and grabbed their rifles.

For one terrifying moment, the soldiers stood rooted to the ground with fear as they looked up in the early morning light and saw the huge war party towering above them. Warriors and ponies were daubed with war paint. The experienced warriors with battle honors wore their prized warbonnets and war shirts, while the rest were stripped down to breechclouts. Lances, bows, tomahawks, and rifles were held motionless above their heads while they waited the command to attack. It came seconds later, a terrible blood-curdling war whoop from the six hundred throats in unison.

Major Forsyth yelled the order for carbines at the ready. As the whooping Indians raced down on the little band of men, he gave the command to fire. The concentrated fire from the Spencers slowed down the charge momentarily, because the Indians had not expected such a barrage of bullets. In that brief respite, Forsyth ordered his men to mount and ride for the island.

THE BATTLE OF BEECHER'S ISLAND

The soldiers made for the island, the war-cries of the Indians ringing in their ears.

The little island was in the center of the river about 75 yards from the bank. Because of a dry summer, the river was only a few inches deep. Amid the wild yells of the Indians milling around to attack, the soldiers raced towards the island, without stopping to take their food, provisions, or medical supplies.

Gaining the island, they formed a circle with their mounts, which they tied to the bushes. Forsyth, Beecher, McCall, and Grover flung themselves down in the long grass, and kept up a steady fire. Meanwhile the rest of the party began frantically scooping out the sandy soil to dig rifle pits large enough to protect their bodies from the flying bullets.

The enemy seemed to be everywhere, firing as they charged the island in an attempt to kill the soldiers at close quarters. Under Forsyth's orders, a hail of bullets from the soldier's repeating rifles broke the wall of mounted warriors. They were forced to part and gallop down both sides of the island and beyond it.

The Indians regrouped and charged. Again they were driven back by the devastating fire from the Spencers. Although Forsyth was hit in the first violent attack, he calmed and encouraged his men. All their horses had been killed, and for added protection the soldiers used them to barricade their rifle pits.

The fight was just beginning. Sitting on the crest of the hill overlooking the small island was one of the great Cheyenne warriors. He was tall, handsome, and muscular. Known as Bat to his tribe and his enemies, he was called Roman Nose by white settlers and soldiers because his nose was hooked.

The Cheyennes believed that this famous warrior had a charmed life, since the arrows and bullets never touched him. He could ride through heavy fire without being hit. Roman Nose believed that his protection came from his sacred warbonnet, which he always wore in battle. The power of the headdress, however, depended on his obeying certain taboos. If disregarded, these taboos could take away the warbonnet's protective powers.

The night before the battle, Roman Nose had unknowingly violated one of the taboos. There had been no time for a ceremony of purification to restore the protective power to the warbonnet. One taboo was not to eat any food prepared or touched by an iron instrument. He had been invited by the Sioux to a feast, and too late he found out that the squaw who had cooked the meal had used an iron fork. He knew that if he donned his warbonnet and entered the fight, he would be killed. But he was a fighting chief of great courage; he would lead his warriors in the next attack.

And so it was that the mighty Roman Nose, mounted on a huge chestnut war pony, took his place at the head of his warriors. He wore his magnificent plumed warbonnet and brandished a rifle over his head. With a deep-throated battle cry, followed by a roar from hundreds of Indians, he led the massed warriors in a death-defying charge.

Fear gripped the little band of soldiers as they saw the formidable enemy charging down on them from all sides. They had recognized Roman Nose, but they remained steady and waited until the Indians were fifty yards away before opening fire.

At Forsyth's command, the soldiers fired as one man. A wall of bullets smashed into the Indians, downing men and horses. But the waves of Indians kept coming. A second volley poured from the Spencers, then a third, and a fourth. As the riders and horses fell, those behind leapt over them. A fifth volley brought gaps in the Indians' ranks, and their horses floundered in the water. Roman Nose, the plumes of his warbonnet streaming out behind him, led his warriors closer and closer to the sweating soldiers, whose repeaters were pouring bullet after bullet into the charging Indians.

Forsyth was hit again and so was Lt. Beecher and the surgeon, Dr. Mooers. But the gallant soldiers never faltered. Forsyth looked up through pain-filled eyes and saw that Roman Nose was only ten yards away. Then suddenly it happened. A bullet from one of the soldier's Spencers smashed into him, and the mighty warrior and his mount crashed down in the shallow, muddy water. The medicine of Roman Nose was broken forever.

Forsyth's men remained steady and waited calmly for their leader to give the signal before opening fire.

As the soldiers watched, the startled Indians faltered and reined in their mounts. Those closest to their dead war chief dragged him out of the water and carried him away, while the others fired half-hearted volleys at the white men. They then veered round and rode off in confusion and despair. With no Roman Nose to lead them, all fight went out of the Indians.

Abner "Sharp" Grover said it was the most violent Indian attack he had ever experienced. Seven soldiers were dead, including Lt. Beecher and Dr. Mooers, and sixteen had been wounded. Forsyth had been shot in the thigh, his left leg was broken below the knee, and he had a bullet wound in his head.

The Indians did not charge again, but they kept the soldiers under siege with long-range sniping. Forsyth asked for four volunteers to try to get help from Fort Wallace, about 10 miles away. The soldiers had to sneak through the Indian lines. Then to avoid any Indian scouts, they walked on foot by night and rested by day. They set off in pairs within two days of each other.

The besieged troop knew that if one of the four men was able to reach Fort Wallace, it would be well over a week before help could arrive. With four able-bodied men gone, the little band was almost defenseless. Major Forsyth urged those who were not wounded to try to get away, but they would not desert their gallant commander or their comrades.

Sandy Forsyth was in such agony with his thigh he was forced to cut out the bullet himself with his knife, gritting his teeth against the terrible pain.

On the hilltop, the Indians were waiting and watching for the soldiers to die, either from their wounds or from starvation. Had they attacked again the soldiers could not have held them off. But the warriors were so stunned by the death of Roman Nose they had no wish to continue the fight.

The soldiers held on with grim determination. Somehow they had to stay alive. They had no food and existed on a few berries and rotting horseflesh, which they seasoned with gunpowder to try to make it edible.

Nine days later Abner "Sharp" Grover, who was acting sentry, let out a hoarse cry. Reinforcements had arrived. All four soldiers had made it to Fort Wallace. Captain Louis H. Carpenter rode in with two troops of the 10th Cavalry just in time to save Forsyth and his men. The 10th Cavalry was one of four black regiments that fought in the Indian wars.

Major Forsyth and his men decided to name the island after young Lt. Beecher, who had been the first to die during the battle.

Forsyth's idea of a small band of mobile men did not turn out to be the solution he envisioned. They did not conquer the warring Indians, but at least he and his troop of valiant men had done their best in trying out the idea. They had been outnumbered twenty to one. Half their number had been killed or wounded, and they had been stranded without food and medical supplies, yet they had held the Indians at bay and had not surrendered.

The story of Forsyth and the Battle of Beecher's Island was told countless times in army posts and around campfires all across the

Led by Captain Louis H. Carpenter, two troops of the 10th Cavalry charged the Indians just in time to save Forsyth and his men. The Indians turned and fled.

Forsyth and his men were outnumbered twenty to one but they had not surrendered.

Plains. Newspapers across the country reported the heroic action.

The action itself was not significant as battles go. Incredibly, only nine Indians had been killed. There were many wounded, but it was the horses that were killed in great numbers. Yet the Battle of Beecher's Island was one of the most honored and glorified in the history of the Indian-Fighting Army.

TWO GALLANT MEN

In a hot June day in 1877, warriors of the Nez Perce tribe ambushed two troops of the lst Cavalry in a canyon in Idaho.

The troopers were outnumbered eight to one. Their sergeant, Michael McCarthy, hurriedly called six of his men to follow him up a rocky slope. They dismounted, grabbed their repeating rifles, and poured rapid fire into the charging warriors.

The Indian attack was so fierce that the rest of the troopers were forced to retreat. Sergeant McCarthy and his men were left to fend for themselves. With Indian warriors swarming all around, uttering hideous war cries, the little band of cavalrymen somehow managed to mount up and fight their way through the yelling Indians. When their ammunition gave out, they used their rifle butts as clubs or slashed at the warriors with their knives.

Two troopers were killed, and the sergeant's horse was shot out from under him. He leapt on to a riderless horse but that, too, was killed. By this time McCarthy had become separated from his men. Horseless, he took refuge in a clump of bushes and laid low. Luck was with the remaining four troopers who raced to safety.

While waiting for a chance to escape, McCarthy saw a war party heading his way. At the same time he noticed, to his horror, that his boots were sticking out of the bush under which he was taking cover. To move his legs might attract the attention of the Indians. Instead he rapidly slipped off his boots, left them where they were and crawled deeper into the bushes.

He waited until nightfall. Then he crept into the hills and headed for his camp. Three days later, tired, hungry, and thirsty, with sore and bleeding feet, he reached his company. For his bravery in action, Sergeant McCarthy was awarded the Medal of Honor.

Only 416 soldiers won the army's highest award during all the years of the Indian-Fighting Army. No man above the rank of major was given this decoration, not even General George Armstrong Custer.

Another unsung hero who was awarded the Medal of Honor for valor was Private Jeremiah J. Murphy of the 3rd Cavalry.

It was March 1876, and the village of Crazy Horse, the mighty Sioux chieftain, was under attack.

Murphy, with five other soldiers, was ordered to form a picket line. The angry Sioux warriors immediately broke through the line,

The little band of cavalrymen mounted and fought their way through the howling Indians. McCarthy's horse was shot from under him and the sergeant fell headlong.

and Murphy and his tiny force found themselves cut off from the rest of the column.

Valiantly the troopers tried to fight their way through the encircling Indians, but four were killed and one was badly wounded. Murphy was about to make a final run for safety when he heard the wounded soldier cry out to him to be saved.

As Murphy turned to hoist the wounded man onto his shoulder a bullet smashed the butt of his carbine. Facing a hail of bullets from the Sioux's rifles, he tried to run on foot for the shelter of some trees. But one of the bullets hit his wounded comrade and killed him.

George Armstrong Custer, the long-haired young general as he looked during the Civil War, twelve years before his last battle.

Murphy laid him on the ground. Then before the warriors realized what he was up to, he raced through their ranks and managed to reach the column. Parts of his uniform were torn by bullet holes but, to the amazement of his company who had watched his dash to safety, he was unhurt.

The courageous young private deserved his Medal of Honor.

THE BOY GENERAL

Lieutenant Colonel George Armstrong Custer was making history when, riding at the head of the 7th Cavalry, he led his gallant regiment to the Battle of the Little Big Horn.

The intrepid officer wore a kerchief knotted casually at his neck and a broad-brimmed hat on his fair hair. He turned in his saddle, his eyes shining with pride as he looked back at his regiment.

The 7th Cavalry was made up of twelve troops. It was Custer's idea to have the horses of each troop of the same color, and the bays, sorrels, blacks, chestnuts, and greys made a colorful pattern as they trotted rhythmically along to the singing of "Garry Owen," the regimental battle song.

With standards and guidons fluttering proudly, six hundred men in army blue set out to fight over three thousand Sioux and Cheyenne warriors on the warpath. They were armed with carbines and revolvers. No saber scabbards hung against the yellow stripes of their blue breeches. Sabers had been ruled out as obsolete weapons. They were considered useless against bullets, and their clatter could betray a surprise attack.

Custer's men were armed only with single-shot Springfield rifles, while the Indians had repeating rifles which they bought from traders. Moreover the cartridge cases of the Springfields were soft and frequently stuck in the overheated breeches. If these facts worried the brilliant commander, his anxiety did not show in his face.

Forty percent of the regiment were recruits, and thirteen of his officers were detailed for other duties. Yet Custer had trained his men well. The 7th was considered one of the finest cavalry units in the United States, and he was confident it would stand up against any Indian attack. It had already done so many times since he had taken command.

George Armstrong Custer was an impetuous, glory-seeking cavalry officer. His career in the Civil War was outstanding, and at twenty-two he was a Major General. Because he was so young, he was referred to as the Boy General. He was utterly fearless and was commended for gallantry five times. At the end of the Civil War he joined the Indian-Fighting Army and was given command of the 7th Cavalry. Like all the high-ranking officers of the Civil War, he had to revert to a lower rank. He went in as a captain but was soon promoted to lieutenant-colonel. He was tall and handsome and wore his hair long. The Indians named him "Yellow Hair."

Custer was called "The Last of the Cavaliers" because of his love of pomp and ceremony, rolling drums, blaring trumpets and flashing sabers. He liked wearing fringed buckskins and rode thoroughbred Kentucky horses. Whenever possible, his big hunting dogs loped along on either side of his mount.

He was an impatient young man who hated following discipline but who was very strict in enforcing it on those under his command. His

Custer led his men out of Fort Lincoln determined to find and fight the Indians. Little did he know that three thousand Indians were waiting for him. Death, too, awaited him.

biggest fault was that he was overeager for action, and he was known several times to disobey orders. In fact, when he was not in the thick of a battle, he was in the thick of trouble. A cavalry brigade once mutinied under his harsh discipline and court-martials and warnings were common events in his career.

Custer never lost an opportunity to win glory, and call attention to himself. On one occasion, in 1878, he had trumped up an excuse for attacking a peaceful camp of Southern Cheyennes that had been set up, under their chief Black Kettle, on the banks of the Washita River.

He had convinced General Philip Sheridan that the Indians were about to take to the warpath, and Sheridan had ordered him to destroy the Cheyenne camp, kill all the warriors and ponies, and bring back the women and children as prisoners.

Custer carried out this merciless order to the letter. Cautiously he led the troopers through a snowstorm and arrived just outside the Cheyenne camp without being seen because of the blinding snow. Impatiently he waited throughout the long night and then, at dawn on a bitterly cold day, he attacked the sleeping camp. His cavalrymen slew more than a hundred warriors, including their chief, as well as many women and children whose lifeless bodies were never counted. Then they burned every lodge, slaughtered hundreds of ponies, and marched those few men, women, and children still left alive back through knee-deep snow to captivity.

Custer had noticed that a few Cheyennes had managed to make good their escape, so before leaving for Fort Dodge, he ordered Major Joel Elliott and eighteen troopers to pursue the lucky few and capture them. Unfortunately Elliott and his men were all slain by furious Indians from nearby encampments.

Impatiently, Custer waited throughout the long night. It was dawn when he ordered his men to attack the sleeping Cheyenne camp. His orders were to kill all the warriors and their ponies.

The men of the 7th Cavalry slew more than a hundred warriors as well as women and children.

Nevertheless, Custer reckoned he had won a great victory. In fact, he had signed his own death warrant. Eight years later, a combined force of Cheyennes and Sioux, all hungry for revenge, were to overwhelm him and his men on the banks of another river, one that is written large in the records of the 7th Cavalry – the Little Big Horn.

It was as the over-proud George Armstrong Custer led his regiment towards the scene of his last battle that he must have reminded himself of the fact that he had very nearly missed leading his regiment into action. He had offended President Grant by accusing his government of corruption. The angry President had forbidden him to take part in the expedition to the Little Big Horn, but Generals Sheridan and Terry had asked the President to reconsider his decision. At the last moment, Grant had given his permission for the reckless, courageous officer to rejoin his regiment.

And so it was that on that particular day in June 1876, this dashing cavalier of the Plains, riding a Kentucky thoroughbred named Vic, led his regiment to the junction of the Yellowstone and Rosebud Rivers. There on a supply ship called the "Far West," Custer met General Terry and Colonel Gibbon to draw up a final campaign of action against the Indians.

GLORY HUNTING

The Sioux and Cheyenne warriors had taken the warpath because the Sioux treaty had been broken. White settlers were flocking to their territory in the Black Hills in search of gold. The Indian could no longer depend upon the word of his white brother. His lands and his buffalo were being taken away from him, and the Indian had only one recourse: war. The warriors were under the leadership of Sitting Bull, Crazy Horse, Rain-in-the-Face, Gall, and other noted chiefs.

Custer's orders were to meet Terry's and Gibbon's troops on June 26 at a point on the Little Big Horn River. The three columns would then close in on the Sioux and bottle them up in the Little Big Horn Valley.

General Terry gave Custer definite instructions not to follow the Indian trail if it led to the valley of the Little Big Horn. He was to turn south and wait for the other two columns to join him, and only then the attack would commence.

Before the 7th Cavalry set off on the last trail, General Terry reviewed the troops. This time the band would not be playing them into battle, but the massed trumpeters blew a stirring march. Custer's own headquarters flag, red and blue with silver crossed sabers, flew alongside the regimental standard carried by the color sergeants. As Custer turned in his saddle to salute Terry and Gibbon, they wished him good luck and the Colonel called out: "Now, Custer, don't be greedy, but wait for us."

Custer shouted back as he waved: "No, I won't." Custer's reply, of course, could be

The 7th Cavalry with Custer in the lead took the broad trail towards the Little Big Horn River.

taken either way. Did he mean that he would not be greedy for battle, or that he would not wait for the other two officers' troops to join him?

Custer pushed his men hard, riding thirty miles a day and sometimes more. The heat and the grueling pace caused blisters to form and split on the legs of the troopers. The horses began to suffer from sores caused by sweat under their saddles.

He advanced along an Indian trail leading west towards the Big Horn Mountains. His scouts reported hundreds of Indians on the move. When they reached the point where they were to wait for the troops of Terry and Gibbon, Custer's impatience got the better of him. He was early because he had imposed forced marches. Instead of waiting for the other officers and their men, he gave the signal "Forward, march."

He led his 7th down the broad trail toward the valley of the Little Big Horn, deliberately disobeying his general's orders. He saw before him the chance for a great victory, which would bring triumph and glory for himself and his regiment. He could not resist taking that chance.

Custer's rash action turned the Battle of the Little Big Horn into the greatest of all Indian victories and the worst of all army defeats at the hands of the Indians.

Quietly the Indians waited for the arrival of the doomed soldiers.

Custer's scout, Curley, a Crow Indian. It was he who took back the news of the disaster.

The 7th approached the fork of the Rosebud and Little Big Horn Rivers. In that Montana valley, unknown to Custer, was a village of ten thousand Sioux and Cheyennes, over three thousand of them fighting warriors. He and his six hundred men were surrounded by Indians who had closed in behind them.

Because he was ahead of schedule, help from Terry and Gibbon could not be expected for at least another day. His men and their horses were exhausted. Again and again his scouts warned him to turn back because there were too many Indians. Each time Custer retorted that there were not too many Indians on the whole of the North American continent for the 7th Cavalry to handle. In fact, the size of the Indian force made him more eager to fight. The greater the number he defeated, the greater would be the fame of his victory. Perhaps had he known that the strength of the Indian force was three thousand warriors, he might not have rushed so eagerly into battle.

The headstrong commander gave his officers their battle orders. He divided the regiment into three. Five troops, two hundred and eleven men, were to accompany him. Three

On the banks of the Little Big Horn, Custer and his two hundred and eleven troopers died to a man. Not one lived to tell the story of Custer's last stand.

troops were to go with Major Reno who, although recommended three times for gallantry in action during the Civil War, was not experienced in Indian fighting. Three troops were to accompany Captain Benteen, an older officer who disliked Custer intensely. The twelfth and last troop was to guard the pack train. Some of his officers thought the regiment should not have been split up without the support of Terry's and Gibbon's troops.

The weary but gallant 7th swung into their saddles and moved off.

No soldier lived to tell the story of Custer's last stand. The records we have today have been told by Indian warriors and scouts who, years afterwards, related their experiences.

Custer, doubtless with a glint of war shining in his eyes, led his two hundred and eleven men in a wild charge over the ridge down into the valley below. Crazy Horse, Rain-in-the-Face, and Gall were waiting and ready for the attack. Uttering piercing war cries, hundreds of warriors swarmed around Custer and his men from all sides.

In one brief, terrifying hour it was all over.

The white soldiers were mown down by the Indians' repeater rifles. Desperately the soldiers fired their single-shot Springfields until

they became red hot. The soft cartridge cases jammed in the breeches, as they had been known to do. Many a trooper died while frantically trying to dig out the cases with his knife. The unfortunate troopers never stood a chance against the modern Winchester repeating rifles the Indians were using.

The Sioux and Cheyennes, their faces frighteningly smeared with war paint, fought viciously against the hated white soldiers. For once they had the advantage over them. Repeaters spat, and spiked war clubs rose and fell, smashing the skulls of the soldiers. Dead horses lay all round them.

Custer made his last stand near the summit of a hill, his men grouped around him. He stood there bravely blazing away with his revolver. Within a short time all the ammunition had been used up. The last cartridges had been fired from the red hot carbines. The few men left standing with their commander were killed even as they emptied their revolvers into

The soldiers never stood a chance against the horde of Indian warriors.

Lieutenant Colonel Custer with his wife (seated on his right), his brothers, Boston (in top hat seated on left) and Tom (on right with sombrero and white neckerchief). Standing on Custer's right is Myles Keogh, whose horse Comanche was the only survivor of the massacre.

the hordes of warriors milling round them.

Suddenly, two bullets hit Custer, one in the head and the other in his side. He fell headlong to the ground, surrounded by his dead troopers.

A horrific sight met General Terry and Colonel Gibbon on the morning of June 27. The battlefield was strewn with the bodies of the two hundred and eleven men and their impetuous commander. Many had been scalped and stripped of their uniforms. As the two officers picked their way through the field of dead soldiers and horses they found Custer's body. He had not been scalped.

For a long time the Indians had wanted the scalp of Yellow Hair to add to their collection of trophies. Before setting out on the march, Custer had suddenly decided to have his long hair cut so that he was not recognized by the warriors. It was much later that they learned Yellow Hair had fought there that day.

Through his complete disregard of orders, Custer had unnecessarily sacrificed the lives of his troops, including four of his relatives. His two brothers, Boston and Tom, who was Captain of C Troop (he had been twice awarded the Medal of Honor in the Civil War), his nephew, Henry Armstrong Reed, and his brother-in-law, Lieutenant James Calhoun of L Troop, were all killed on that fatal day.

Captain Benteen and Major Reno had fought bravely and well and were later given promotions. Forty-seven of Reno's men had been killed and fifty-three wounded.

There was just one survivor of that terrible battle. It was Comanche, a beautiful charger that belonged to Captain Myles Keogh, a pleasant, laughing Irish officer, liked by all his **fellow officers and men. Comanche was severely wounded and was found standing over** the dead body of its master. The faithful horse was taken away and looked after. In time it recovered from its wounds, but it was never ridden again, except on ceremonial occasions. It died at the age of 28 in 1891.

What a story the horse could have told if only it could have talked.

SOLDIERS OF THE FRONTIER

The men who manned the lonely army posts on the frontier were volunteers. They came from all walks of life. Some wanted excitement and glory; others wanted to travel and see the West. There were those who wanted to escape from working on farms and those who needed a job. Some volunteers were criminals avoiding capture who changed their names. Some were immigrants from Europe who could barely speak English. Men joined up for every reason under the sun.

The life the volunteers chose was hard, tough, and often brutal.

Soldiers out on campaigns spent hours in the saddle or on foot, always alert, ready to grab their carbines at the first sign of Indians. Revolvers nestled in holsters on their right hips, and sheath knives hung from their belts.

Sabers were usually left behind at the garrison. A surprise night attack could be spoiled by their telltale "clanking," a sure sign of approaching soldiers. Sabers were cumbersome weapons, but many a cavalryman, fighting for his life, wished his saber was at hand when his ammunition had given out and he was engaged in hand-to-hand combat with the enemy.

Infantrymen, too, left their bayonets behind, preferring to use their knives when their guns became useless.

Army rations were poor. "Forty miles a day on beans and hay" was a favorite joke. In those days there were no trained cooks. Most of the men who prepared the meals knew nothing about cooking. Another joke among the men was that the cooks killed more soldiers than the Indians did. Beans, hardtack, greasy salt pork, and coffee formed their staple diet.

Soldiers had to survive and fight in appalling weather conditions, from freezing blizzards and deep snow to merciless heat and burning sun. In the early years of the Frontier Army, the uniforms were not warm enough to keep out the intense cold. In the summer heat, the same uniforms were too hot.

Men in the Indian-Fighting Army had many duties besides fighting battles against the warring Indian tribes. Troops were sent throughout the vast territory of the west from the Mississippi River to the Pacific Ocean. They protected miners, settlers, and cattle ranchers. They surveyed railroad lines and guarded the construction crews, since there was always the threat of an Indian attack. They escorted and protected wagon trains and kept the main trails or routes open and free of war parties. They built bridges and repaired telegraph lines, which the Indians called "whispering wires" and frequently pulled down. The soldiers did any job that was required of them and did it well.

Some of the most reliable soldiers were black. They served in four regiments under white officers. They fought hard, seldom deserted, and were well disciplined. The Indians they fought respected them and called them "Buffalo Soldiers." They saw a resemblance between the curly hair of the black soldiers and the buffalo's shaggy coat. The Plains Indians considered the buffalo a sacred animal and were honoring the black soldiers by giving them that name.

Discipline in the Frontier Army was harsh. Men who committed small offenses such as oversleeping and missing roll call were fined a month's pay or

Army rations were poor. In this photograph, four troopers make the best of a meal of beans and salt pork washed down with scalding hot coffee.

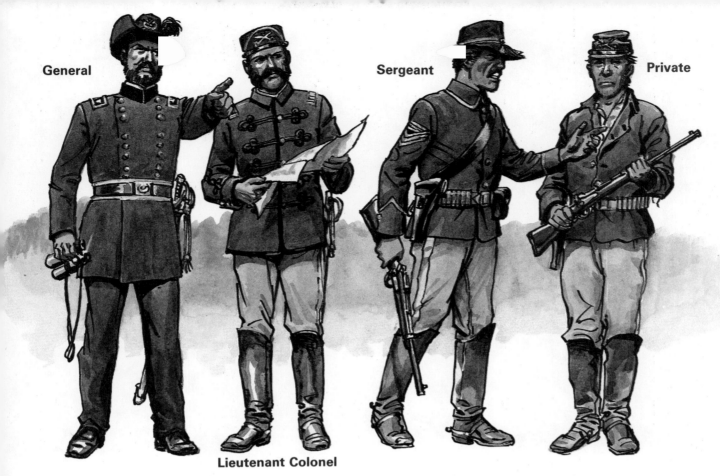

General

Sergeant

Private

Lieutenant Colonel

confined to the guardhouse for a month – or both.

General Custer was particularly severe with the men under his command. He designed a special guardhouse. It was a 15-foot deep hole in the ground covered with boards. Soldiers imprisoned down there for minor offenses must have felt their punishment was very harsh indeed.

A soldier found drunk or disorderly might have been ordered to march all day, in all weathers, carrying a 30- to 40-pound log. If a soldier deserted and was captured, he would have to wear a 25-pound ball and chain around his ankle for weeks or even months, like a convict in a chain gang.

This sort of punishment was responsible for the desertion of a third of all the soldiers recruited during the Indian wars. Many wished they had not been so eager to volunteer.

Soldiers normally spent half their time on campaigns against the Indians and the rest of the time at an army post. They were glad to have a rest from long marches and fighting, but there were no home comforts in a fort.

In the 1860s forts or army posts were built of whatever material was available, usually wood, adobe, or logs mixed with sand, mud, and lime. To protect the garrison from sudden Indian attacks, since danger was never far away, high fences made of strong wooden stakes surrounded the buildings. These fences were called palisades or stockades. The fort gates were shut and barred at night, and sentries were posted along the top of the stockade. People living inside the enclosed fort felt safe and protected.

A fort had to have enough water for a regiment or several companies and grass for the horses. It usually contained a barracks, storehouses, stables, workshop, guardhouse, officers' quarters, married quarters, and a parade ground. Some forts had a blacksmith and a trading post.

A few officers and enlisted men were allowed to have their wives and children with them. The quarters where the soldiers and their wives lived was known as "Suds Row" or "Sudsville," because some of the wives did the laundry for the garrison. For this work they were paid from two to five dollars a month. Washing was hard work, but the "laundry ladies," as they were called, were only too pleased to earn a few dollars to supplement their husbands' pay. Soldiers were poorly paid.

The fort was a busy place. Bugle calls sounded all through the day, summoning the men to various duties. These included drills on the parade ground, barracks inspection, and guard duty. Horses had to be groomed, watered, and exercised. Men were detailed to cut wood for fuel and to bring in water. The parade ground had to be swept and the buildings kept clean. While these and other duties were being carried out, the soldiers always had to stay on the alert for any sudden attack by a war party.

Some of the small army camps scattered across the Plains were made of log huts and tents. These were usually infested with rats, mice, and insects. Living conditions in the small camps were even rougher than in the larger forts.

Whether in a large camp or small, it was a tough life for an army man on the frontier.

IN THE DAYS OF THE INDIANS

1680-1692   The Pueblo Indians of the Southwest revolt against the Spanish rule.

1689-1763   The French and Indian Wars are fought between France and Britain for possession of North America.

1784   The Iroquois Indians of New York are forced to cede all their lands west of the Niagara River.

1800   The Cherokee Indians of the mid-Atlantic states adopt some ways of the whites. They begin plantations and own slaves. They establish a Republican form of government called the Cherokee nation.

1821   Sequoya, a Cherokee Indian, invents a system of writing for the Cherokee language.

1824   Fur trappers enter the Northwest Territory to hunt, and disagreements arise with the local Indians.

1830   Congress passes the Indian Removal Act forcing all Indians living east of the Mississippi River to give up their lands and move west.

1837   Osceola, chief of the Seminole tribe in Florida, is captured. The Seminole Wars end with the tribe nearly wiped out.

1838-1839   The Cherokee Indians begin their long journey on foot to the Oklahoma Territory. Many die along the way. The forced march is known as the "Trail of Tears."

1861   The Civil War begins over the issue of slavery.

1861-1900   The Apache Wars begin during the Civil War. Cochise and Geronimo are two chiefs who lead raids on outposts in the southwest.

1865   President Lincoln is assassinated and the Civil War ends.

1866   Indians are forced to cede half of Oklahoma to white settlers.

1874   Gold is discovered in the Black Hills of South Dakota. Fighting breaks out between the Sioux and whites looking for gold.

1876   General George Armstrong Custer and over two hundred men are wiped out by the Sioux in retaliation for the Sioux defeat at Little Big Horn, Montana. It is called "Custer's Last Stand."

1889   The Sioux are forced to cede 9,000,000 acres to the government.

1890   The Dakota Sioux stage the "Ghost Dance War."

1890   The Sioux Wars end. Great chiefs like Sitting Bull and Crazy Horse are either dead or captured.

1890   Oklahoma is organized as a territory.

1894   The end of the Red River War between the army and the Arapaho and Cheyenne of the Southern Plains.

IN THE DAYS OF THE PIONEERS

1492	Christopher Columbus discovers America.
1540-1542	Francisco Vasquez de Coronado explores the territory which is now New Mexico and Arizona. He is searching for seven fabled cities of gold to claim for Spain.
1669-1673	Rene Robert Cavelier (La Salle) becomes the first European to explore the Mississippi River to the Gulf of Mexico. He names it Louisiana, in honor of King Louis, and claims it for France.
1513	Vasco Nunez de Balboa becomes the first European to see the Pacific Ocean from what is now Panama. He claims Panama and the surrounding territory for Spain.
1690-1770	Texas and California become Spanish strongholds.
1776	The Declaration of Independence is signed.
1803	The U.S. buys Louisiana from France for $15,000,000.
1804	Meriwether Lewis and William Clark embark on the first expedition by the U.S. Government to explore the Northwest Territory.
1824-1830	Fur trappers arrive in the newly mapped Northwest Territory to hunt for pelts.
1775	Daniel Boone blazes the Wilderness Trail from North Carolina to Kentucky and founds Boonesborough, Kentucky.
1806	Zebulon Pike explores Colorado.
1825	The opening of the Erie Canal makes transportation to the west coast easier.
1849	Gold is discovered in California and the western rush is on.
1850	California becomes a state.
1850	New Mexico and Utah become territories.
1853	Washington becomes a territory.
1854	Kansas and Nebraska become territories.
1859	Oregon becomes a state.
1862	The Homestead Act gives 160 acres of western land to anyone who agrees to settle on it.
1867	Nebraska becomes a state.
1868	Wyoming is organized as a territory.
1876	Colorado becomes a state.
1889-1893	Treaties with Indians are ignored. Settlers flock to Indian lands in Oklahoma.
1892	Commodore Peary explores the Arctic.
1897	The discovery of gold in Alaska causes a rush to the Klondike.
1898	Hawaii is annexed to the U.S.

IN THE DAYS OF THE COWBOYS

1521	Cattle are brought to Mexico by the Spanish.
1775	Daniel Boone carves out the Wilderness Trail from North Carolina to Kentucky, opening new land for settlement.
1800	The Harrison Land Act allows private individuals to stake claims to lands in the western territories.
1808	Congress forbids the importation of more slaves.
1816	James Monroe is elected president.
1823	The Monroe Doctrine states that the Western Hemisphere is no longer open to European colonization.
1829	William Lloyd Garrison proposes the immediate end to slavery in his work Genius of Universal Emancipation.
1830	The Indian Removal Act forces all Indians living east of the Mississippi to give up their lands and move west.
1859	A large deposit of gold, called the Comstock Lode, is discovered in Nevada.
1862	Richard Gatling designs a revolving machine gun.
1862	Julia Ward Howe writes the "Battle Hymn of the Republic."
1862	The Homestead Act grants 160 acres of western land to anyone who will settle and cultivate it. Wide open spaces where cattle roam become fenced in farmland.
1864	Nevada becomes a state and Montana is organized as a territory.
1866	Cattle drives begin from Texas to Kansas/Nebraska and beyond. These ordeals are known as the "long drives."
1869	Wyoming is the first state to give women the right to vote.
1876	Alexander Graham Bell invents the telephone.
1877	The first black man graduates from West Point.
1880	Gold is discovered in Alaska.
1880	James A. Garfield is elected president.
1881	Garfield is assassinated and his vice-president, Chester Arthur succeeds him.
1892	The General Electric Company is formed.
1893	Henry Ford builds his first automobile.
1896	Motion pictures are invented.
1896	The Supreme Court legalizes segregation. The case of Plessy vs. Ferguson establishes a "separate but equal" doctrine.
1899	John Dewey puts forth his theories on education in The School and Society.
1900	William McKinley is elected president.
1901	McKinley is assassinated and succeeded by his vice-president, Theodore Roosevelt.
1929	The Rodeo Association of America is started.

IN THE DAYS OF THE RAILROADERS

1700's   A simple wooden rail is used to carry coal from underground to the surface in Britain.

1804   Richard Trevithick, an English engineer, builds the first steam engine.

1825   George Stephenson, another English engineer, opens the first railroad ever to carry passengers.

1825   The Erie Canal opens. It takes eight years and $7,000,000 to cover the 362 miles the canal spans. It is a momentous undertaking and an important link between the east and west coasts.

1830   Stephenson builds the Rocket, the first steam engine.

1835   Over 200 railroad charters exist in eleven states.

1848-1849   The California gold rush points up the need for faster transportation to the west.

1850   Congress allows special grants of land to railroad owners to promote settlement of the western territories.

1858   The Southern Overland Mail route begins.

1860   The Pony Express begins a mail run from Missouri to California.

1861   Invented in 1837 by Samuel Morse, the telegraph now links the country from coast to coast.

1862   The Pacific Railroad Act gives two private companies huge tracts of land and millions of dollars to build a railroad to attract settlers to the western states.

1863   Locomotive engineers organize the first successful railroad union.

1864   Regular railway mail begins service.

1864   The Northern Pacific Railroad is chartered.

1869   The tracks of the Central Pacific and Union Pacific are joined at Promontory, Utah, to form the Transcontinental Railroad.

1874   Jesse James and his gang begin robbing trains.

1880   According to a treaty with China, the United States has the right to regulate Chinese immigration. Chinese are used as laborers by the railroad companies.

1881   People of many occupations band together under one union, the Federation of Organized Trades and Labor Unions.

1882   Labor Day is first celebrated.

1882   Congress passes the Exclusion Act which bars further Chinese immigration.

1895   The Baltimore and Ohio Railroad begins the world's first electric main line service.

1897   Boston begins the first subway.

1900   The Wright Brothers build the first glider.

1934   The Zephyr, the first electric passenger train, begins service.

1964   The Japanese invent passenger trains that can travel at speeds of 130 MPH.

IN THE DAYS OF THE GUNFIGHTERS

1730's	Horses are introduced into the plains, where they flourish. They spread into Canada. Many Indian tribes adopt ponies for transportation and buffalo hunting.
1776	The Declaration of Independence is signed.
1783	The Revolutionary War with Britain comes to an end when the final peace treaty is signed on September 3.
1812	Britain attempts to reclaim the American colonies. The White House is burned. The attempt ends in failure.
1831	Alexis De Tocqueville, a Frenchman, comes to America to explore the new nation. His book, Democracy in America, is a study of the society and politics of the time.
1836	Arkansas becomes a state.
1836	Martin Van Buren is elected president.
1837	Michigan becomes a state and Minnesota is organized as a territory.
1837	The telegraph is invented by Samuel Morse. Morse is also a portrait painter.
1837-1901	The reign of Queen Victoria of Britain.
1855	The Free Soil convention drafts an anti-slavery constitution.
1858	The first stage coach line to the west coast begins. It originates in St. Louis.
1860	The Pony Express begins a mail run from Missouri to California.
1861	Abraham Lincoln is elected president.
1861	Confederates fire on Fort Sumter, beginning the Civil War. In the south it is called the War Between The States.
1861	The telegraph links the country from east coast to west coast.
1862	The Homestead Act encourages settlement in the west, closing the wide open spaces.
1865	General Lee, leader of the Confederate army, surrenders to General Ulysses S. Grant, leader of the Union army. They meet at Appomattox on April 9. The Civil War ends.
1865	President Lincoln is assassinated at Ford's Theatre on April 14.
1874	The James/Younger gang begins robbing trains.
1881	The governor of New Mexico, Lew Wallace, signs Billy the Kid's death warrant.
1900	The census finds the population of the U.S. is a little over 75,000,000.
1900	The Wright Brothers build their first glider.
1901	Oil is discovered in Texas, causing a boom in that state.
1902	Buffalo Bill takes his Wild West show to Great Britain, where it is a huge success.

IN THE DAYS OF THE SOLDIERS

1754-1763	The French and Indian War gives Great Britain the advantage in North America.
1769	James Watt invents the first steam engine.
1773	The Boston Tea Party.
1774	The Minutemen are organized. They are pro-independence soldiers who are trained to fight the British at a minute's notice.
1775	The battle of Lexington and Concord begins the Revolutionary War.
1776	The Declaration of Independence is signed, formalizing the American commitment to freedom.
1783	The Treaty of Paris ends the Revolutionary War.
1789	George Washington, hero of the Revolution, becomes the first president.
1789	Inspired by America's successful war for independence, revolution breaks out in France.
1812-1814	Britain tries to regain her lost American colonies, resulting in the War of 1812.
1815	The Treaty of Ghent ends the War of 1812.
1823	President James Monroe formulates the Monroe Doctrine which states that the western hemisphere is no longer open to European colonization.
1836	Texas wins independence from Mexico with the Battle of the Alamo.
1852	Harriet Beecher Stowe writes Uncle Tom's Cabin.
1854	Passage of the Kansas-Nebraska Act increases tensions on the slavery issue.
1854	Abraham Lincoln and Stephen Douglas debate the issue of slavery.
1859	John Brown's raid on Harper's Ferry.
1861	Lincoln is elected president on an anti-slavery platform.
1861	Confederate troops attack Fort Sumter, beginning the Civil War.
1861	The Battle of Bull Run. Northern troops are defeated. General Robert E. Lee distinguishes himself and becomes leader of the Confederacy.
1863	Lincoln issues the Emancipation Proclamation, freeing the slaves.
1864	General Ulysses S. Grant becomes chief of northern forces, later he will become president.
1865	In April, Lee surrenders to Grant at Appomattox, ending the Civil War.
1865	Lincoln is assassinated in Ford's Theatre by John Wilkes Booth.
1865	The Thirteenth Amendment to the Constitution abolishes slavery.
1870	The Fifteenth Amendment to the Constitution gives blacks the right to vote.
1890	Begun in 1861, the Apache Wars finally end with the defeat of the Indian tribe.
1890	After decades of fighting, the Sioux Wars end. Much blood has been shed on both sides.